the PAIN KILLER

FINDING MEANING AFTER MURDER

Greg Hoover

Black Rose Writing | Texas

©2022 by Greg Hoover
All rights reserved. No part of this book may be reproduced, stored in a retrieval system or transmitted in any form or by any means without the prior written permission of the publishers, except by a reviewer who may quote brief passages in a review to be printed in a newspaper, magazine or journal.

The author grants the final approval for this literary material.

First printing

This is a work of fiction. Names, characters, businesses, places, events, and incidents are either the products of the author's imagination or used in a fictitious manner. Any resemblance to actual persons, living or dead, or actual events is purely coincidental.

ISBN: 978-1-68513-021-3
PUBLISHED BY BLACK ROSE WRITING
www.blackrosewriting.com

Printed in the United States of America
Suggested Retail Price (SRP) $20.95

The Pain Killer is printed in Palatino Linotype

*As a planet-friendly publisher, Black Rose Writing does its best to eliminate unnecessary waste to reduce paper usage and energy costs, while never compromising the reading experience. As a result, the final word count vs. page count may not meet common expectations.

Praise for
THE PAIN KILLER

"A cross between true crime and The Shack, Greg Hoover's new book explores the Chicago Tylenol Murders as a springboard to help people find faith, hope, and healing in the face of evil."
–A.J. McCarthy,
award-winning mystery and suspense author

"Part unsolved mystery and part spiritual autobiography, Greg Hoover leads us on a personal journey into God's uncontrolling love."
–Dr. Thomas Jay Oord, theologian, scholar,
and best-selling author

"Greg Hoover's new book is not only a fascinating dramatization of the Tylenol Murders, but also a moving coming-of-age story set in an innocent time, now gone."
–Dan McDowell, author of *Level Zero*

"A riveting and compelling murder mystery based on actual events. More than a mystery novel, this is Greg Hoover's personal journey of self-discovery and spiritual transformation. Fasten your seat belt and prepare to be blown away by this psychological thriller. I certainly was!"
–Joseph J. Luciani, Ph.D., author of
Unlearning Anxiety & Depression

"*The Pain Killer* takes hold from page one and doesn't let go. Highly recommended."
–J.P. Hostetler, author of the *Around Curiosity's Edge* **series**

DEDICATION

This book is dedicated to the victims of the Chicago Tylenol Murders and their families. May their loss never be forgotten. It is also dedicated to the law enforcement officers and FBI agents who worked tirelessly to solve this mystery. It is likewise dedicated to Johnson & Johnson, whose speedy action saved lives. Finally, this book is dedicated to my parents. Your kindness and generosity can never be paid back, so I will do my best to pay it forward. Thank you for keeping us safe.

ACKNOWLEDGEMENTS

So many have helped make this book a reality. The author wishes to thank the Author's Guild legal help department; James Grisham, Esq.; Timothy Davis, Esq.; Dr. Gwen Gresham; Dr. Thomas Jay Oord; Ethan Hoover; Sophia Hoover; my father and mother as the source of most of the early material in this book; all my beta readers; Reagan Rothe; and the entire staff of Black Rose Writing. This book would not be possible without all of your help.

CONTENTS

PROLOGUE - THE TYLENOL MAN

PART I - THE 1970s BEFORE THE CHANGE

1 - UNLEASH THE FUTURE
2 - BURIED SECRET
3 - BEFORE THE NIGHT
4 - SHADOWS ON THE WALL
5 - THE SHAPE OF THINGS TO COME
6 - THE SINS OF CYANIDE
7 - CHILDREN OF BLOOD
8 - HIDE AND SEEK
9 - BACK TO THE LAND
10 - THE MURDER OF RAYMOND WEST
11 - AVENGING ANGELS

PART II - THE 1980s DURING THE CHANGE

12 - SEVEN MORE MURDERS
13 - THE FACELESS FURY
14 - THE GHOST IN THE GLASS
15 - DEAD HUNT
16 - ARMED AND DANGEROUS
17 - HAPPY HALLOWEEN
18 - CAGE THE SPECTOR

PART III - THE 2000s AFTER THE CHANGE

19 - THE RIVER OF PAIN
20 - THE POWERS THAT BE
21 - THE TERRIFYING LOVE OF GOD

EPILOGUE - FORGIVENESS IS THE BEST REVENGE

the PAIN KILLER

*"Understanding does not cure evil,
but it is a definite help, inasmuch as one
can cope with a comprehensible darkness."*
–C.G. Jung

*"Do not be overcome by evil,
but overcome evil with good."*
–Romans 12:21 (ESV)

PROLOGUE
THE TYLENOL MAN

Friday the 13th, October, 1995

A shooting star blazed across the cold October sky. Hickory smoke rose in the night air as we sat around the glowing campfire.

"This brings back wonderful memories," said my mother. She pulled a handmade quilt around her shoulders to keep out the chill. "Back when you kids were little."

Putting another log on the fire, I smiled at her. "Yeah, we did this all the time while we were growing up."

My father loaded his pipe. "Time passes so fast," he said, tapping the tobacco into the bowl. "It seems like only yesterday you were a boy." He looked up at me and smiled. "Now you're a grown man."

The fire glowed in the cold night, radiating warmth and comfort.

"People always say time passes fast," I said, gazing at the flames. "But I think that really means we were totally in the moment at that point of our lives. We didn't dwell in the past or worry about the future. We were in the present, and nowhere else."

My father struck a match, the light glowing on his face as he lit his pipe. "I think you're right." He blew the match out in a cloud of white smoke.

All was quiet except for the crackle of the campfire. After a few moments, I broke the silence.

"Guys, I have something to tell you."

My father puffed on his pipe. "Oh, what's that?"

"I heard something today I think you should know."

My father's pipe glowed as the rich scent of Cavendish filled the air. "What'd you hear?"

Throwing a twig on the fire, I looked at my parents. Tension filled the air.

My mother rubbed her hands together to warm them. "Just say it."

"You remember the Chicago Tylenol Murders that happened back in '82?"

Dad puffed on his pipe. "Oh, yes."

"Well ..."

"Well, what?"

"They released John Price from prison this morning."

Dad sat up straight. "Oh, no. Where'd you hear that?"

"I was at the pharmacy this evening, picking up your medicine," I said. "The workers there were talking about it."

"What did they say?"

"They called him the 'Tylenol Man.' They said he killed all those people, and that he was released from prison this morning."

"Did they ask you about him?" said Dad. His blue eyes were wide. "Do you think they know?"

"I don't think so," I said. "They didn't seem to realize we knew him."

Dad's pipe rested in his hand. "The 'Tylenol Man,'" he said, shaking his head. "That will always be his name now."

Using a metal rake, I repositioned the logs. Sparks rose in the air. "Well, the murders are still unsolved."

"Technically," said Dad.

Mom turned and looked at me. "You were so little when you first met him."

I glanced at Mom. "Five years old."

"Do you have any memories of that time?"

Nodding, I stirred the fire with a long stick. "Oh, yes."

My mind flashed to the image of a grisly crime scene I discovered when I was five. The sights, the smells, the—

"Tell us what you remember," said Mom, her eyes sad and serious. "We'll fill in the gaps in your memories."

Shrugging my shoulders, I looked at Mom. "I was just a small child when it all began." I glanced at my father. "You'll have to do a lot of filling in."

"We will," he said.

Stretching my hands over the fire, I warmed them. "Memories have been flooding back into my mind since I heard the news of his release."

Mom turned to my father. "Harry, I'm afraid. What if he comes back here again?"

"He won't," I said. "I promise. Don't be afraid."

Mom was quiet for a moment and gazed at the flickering campfire. "I think it's good for us to talk about it."

My breath flowed out in a white cloud as I blew on my hands. "Where do we begin?"

Dad dumped his pipe out and put it in his pocket. "Begin at the beginning."

And so we did. We talked late into the night, long after the last embers of our fire had died. Since that night—Friday the 13th, October, 1995—we had dozens of conversations about it. My parents told me so much. They answered many questions I had since childhood. I also researched the murders on my own. Trying to flesh out a full picture, I read dozens of articles, books, and court transcripts. I listened to hours of podcasts, searched my memories, and interviewed my parents and family.

For most people, this story began in 1982, when a great evil happened that changed our world forever. This one event overshadowed all others that year and struck fear into the hearts of every American. An unknown serial killer poisoned Extra Strength Tylenol capsules with potassium cyanide. This safe and popular medication, used daily by millions of people to ease pain and suffering, had become deadly.

Before authorities determined the cause of the sudden deaths, seven people were murdered by cyanide poisoning. When information about the murders hit the news, panic swept through the nation. People were terrified they would be poisoned, too. If something as simple and safe as Tylenol could have been tampered with, then no one was safe. The unknown murderer could have poisoned any medicine, packaged food, or supplement. To complicate matters further, copycat killers soon followed.

My connection to this story starts when I was a five-year-old child and made a grisly discovery. For me, that was the beginning. But this story has expanded into one of the greatest unsolved mass murders in American history. The man with me when I found the hidden secret became infamous. Years later, he was arrested for murder. And years after that, he became the prime suspect in a famous mass murder case that remains unsolved to this day. Perhaps most shocking of all, my parents knew him well. When I was a child, he came to our home. He managed our rental properties for my family. He visited me when I was sick. And to many, he remains the prime suspect in a series of unsolved murders to this day.

This situation has sparked lifelong questions: *What makes a man into a murderer? Why do bad things happen to good people?* And deeper questions have arisen as well: *If God is all-powerful and all good, why is there so much suffering? Is there a psychology of evil? A theology of murder? And how do survivors find meaning after murder?*

This story impacts everyone in the modern world, including the reader. Every time you open a bottle of medicine with a safety seal, or a package of food sealed for your protection, you are connected to this unsolved murder mystery.

My story explores potential connections between the Chicago Tylenol Murders and other crimes. It is about my parent's and family's personal memories and experiences with the prime suspect of the horrible crimes — the same man who was with me when I found the buried secret when I was a child. My story is an inside look recreated from personal experiences and family memories of those events. Moreover, this book explores my lifelong quest to understand the mystery of evil, and to help others find emotional and spiritual healing.

During the Tylenol Murders, the nation watched the news in terror. Americans scrambled to throw away their medicine bottles. Fear gripped the average home as grainy photos of the suspected killer were shown on television. Law enforcement officials struggled to find evidence linking a suspect to the crimes. During all this, the FBI visited our home, interviewed my parents, and searched for their prime suspect. They set up a base near our home and waited for him to arrive. And I was there on the inside, a boy growing into a man, searching for meaning within the madness.

Jack the Ripper is the name society gave to an unknown serial killer in the 1880s. Like the Tylenol murders one hundred years later, that case was never solved. The horrible crimes described in this book were committed by the unknown serial killer some call America's Jack the Ripper. Others call him the Tylenol terrorist. I call him *the Pain Killer*.

This is our story.

PART I
THE 1970s
BEFORE THE CHANGE

1
UNLEASH THE FUTURE

Independence, Missouri, 1971

Life was different then. That was before the change.

When I think back to the moment when the change began, I remember playing quietly in the yard at my home. My new, white tennis shoes, fresh and clean to start kindergarten, glided across the fresh-cut lawn. As I ran through the yard beside our home, I watched the bright white of my new shoes flash through the short green grass. The sweet scent of the fresh-mowed lawn filled the late summer air. The heat was fading and summer would soon pass. The green leaves would change into beautiful red, gold, and orange. Autumn was coming, and with it, another season of innocence. But the change that began the peaceful day would not only alter my life, but the entire world.

Kindergarten would start the following week, so I still had the entire day free to play. It was the early 1970s, and parents knew their young children were safe. We had a remarkable amount of freedom to come and go as we wanted and to explore the world surrounding our home. Sometimes my brothers and I would be gone for hours. We would walk to the local grocery store, wander the quiet neighborhood, or go to the movies. Life was perfect, simple, and sweet.

But that was before the change.

Darren, my oldest brother, was twenty-four years old and out of college. Unlike some of his friends, he hadn't been drafted to fight in Vietnam. Instead, he lived in a small place in Kansas City called *Saint Francis House*. There he, along with a group of similar-minded men and women, sought to live a simple, peaceful, lifestyle.

There was a fifteen-year gap between Darren and Brad, my next oldest brother. Brad was in the Fifth Grade. He was followed by Ed, who was in the Second Grade. My friends called me Jack, and so did my family. I was five years old and excited to start kindergarten soon. My baby sister, Rebecca, was two years old. She was in the house, sleeping. Brad and Ed played with friends at their home. I had the afternoon all to myself.

My favorite ball lay in the yard. I picked it up, glad it was small enough to survive the recent mowing. I bounced the rubber ball on the nearby sidewalk and watched it climb high in the air. A red firetruck pulled up at the stop sign near our home. Two firefighters were riding on the back. One of the men called out to me, "Where's the Captain?"

"He'll be home any minute," I called back.

"Tell your dad we said 'hi,'" said the other man, waving. "Bye Jack!"

"Okay," I shouted and waved back as the truck pulled away. "Bye!"

My father's name was Harold, but my mother always called him Harry. He was the captain of a local fire department in Independence. He would work three days on, followed by three days off. Dad would be home soon, and I always loved to talk to him about his three days at work. Sometimes he would stop by Dunkin' Donuts on his way home. They would give firefighters free donuts, and Dad would often pick up a fresh box for us.

A dove fluttered down and landed on the limb of a nearby tree.

"Bert!" I called out and ran to the tree.

Bert was a dove we rescued and raised to adulthood. Once he was old enough to take care of himself, we set him free. It was always exciting when Bert would come back home to visit.

Brakes squeaked as a car stopped at the stop sign near our house. I glanced over at the car. Three people were in the front seat. A man, a woman, and a little girl about my age. All three turned their heads in unison and looked at me. Then they drove off. I glanced down, and my new white shoes had a light tint of green from the recent mowing.

As Bert flew away, I threw my ball high in the air. Down it came and bounced on the sidewalk. It bounced high at first, and then lower until it came to a rest on the cement. Picking it up, I threw it high in the air again. When it bounced the first time, I saw the same car was back again. Once again, the car came to a stop, and all three people inside turned and looked at me. After a moment, another car pulled up behind them. They didn't seem to notice and kept watching me. The woman moved her lips, saying something I couldn't hear. The car behind them honked. Surprised, they pulled off again.

My yellow bicycle rested against the wall of the garage. I ran over to it and climbed on. Still new to riding, my bike swayed from side to side as I peddled. Soon I had enough speed to make it ride straight, and I kept peddling. *Dad would be home soon*, I thought, *and he'll see how well I'm riding*. As I circled the house on my bike, the scent of the ripe grapes in our garden filled the air.

As I rounded the house a second time, I saw the car again. They pulled up to the stop sign and again turned to look at me. After a moment, they pulled off. I got off my bike and went into our home.

My mother was in the kitchen, wearing a light blue dress and a red apron. Her smile warmed the room. I smiled back and hugged her.

"Mom," I said. "There was a weird car outside."

"What do you mean 'weird'?" she asked as she returned to peeling potatoes.

"I don't know." I shrugged my shoulders. "Just weird."

"You mean it looked weird?"

"No," I said. "It looked regular." I paused and collected my thoughts. "But the people looked weird."

My mother stopped peeling and looked at me. "What did they do?"

"They just keep driving up, and then stopping and looking at me."

"What did they look like?"

"I don't know." I shrugged my shoulders. "A man, a lady, and a little girl."

"And they keep doing it?"

"Uh-huh," I nodded my head.

"Well," she said, turning back to her work. "Why don't you play inside for a while. Sound good?"

The back door of our house opened.

"Dad!" I yelled and ran to him.

"Hey there, little rascal," he said, and tousled my hair with his hand.

"Did you bring donuts?"

"Not today," he said with a smile. "It's almost dinner time."

"Okay," I said. "Maybe next time?"

Dad smiled again. "Maybe."

My father kissed my mother on the cheek. "How was your day, Betty?"

"It was a fine day," she said, and then looked at me. I knew the look well. It was a polite invitation to leave the room. As I turned to leave, I heard my mother say to my father, "Jack said there was a weird car circling the house today …"

***

Dinner was one of my favorites—Meatloaf with potatoes, cooked together to perfection. A glass of cold milk and a slice of homemade cherry pie made a tasty dessert. After dinner, my parents took my little sister and me to their first meeting with a real estate agent. Dad was hoping to augment his salary by buying an inexpensive house. He wanted to fix it up, and either sell or rent it. A friend of my brother Darren gave him the contact information for this realtor. He said this couple could get my family great deals on old houses needing work. Their names were John and Sarah Price.

The Prices did a little of everything. They filed taxes for their clients out of their basement, supplemented their income with freelance bookkeeping, and they sold real estate. And according to Darren's friend, they knew of cheap houses in need of a lot of work. In a phone call, John suggested to my father the idea of buying HUD Houses. These inexpensive houses were available through the Department of Housing and Urban Development (HUD).

"HUD Houses are foreclosed homes that were bought with FHA loans," John had told my father on the phone. "When people default on their loans, the houses are sold off at a reduced price. You can often get several HUD Houses for the price of one regular property."

My parents were cautiously optimistic about this opportunity. As we drove along through the Kansas City traffic, they spoke about what they could do with the extra money.

"If the kids want to go to college someday, maybe we could earn enough to afford it," said my mother as we rode along.

Out the window, we passed billboards hawking goods and services. I thumbed through a Spider-Man comic book my father had bought me. Spider-Man was investigating the bad guys, and something wasn't quite right. There was no evidence, but Peter Parker, Spider-Man's alter ego, felt something was wrong anyway. In the famous words of Peter Parker, "My Spider-Sense is tingling." In the comics, *Spider-Sense* was Peter Parker's intuition working on a high level. It was his super ability to sense danger before it happened. And it became stronger when the threat increased.

My parents chatted about my father's work at the fire department, and a book he was reading.

"That's it," said my father as he pointed out the car window.

My mother glanced at the written directions in her hand. "Yeah, that's it."

We parked our car and walked up to the door. My father knocked, but there was no answer. He glanced at my mother and she shrugged her shoulders. After a moment, he knocked again. This time, we heard whispering inside. After a third knock, a woman's voice called, "Come in."

We entered the room. It was cold and crowded with office equipment. On the walls hung a child's drawings colored with crayons. A little girl with Downs Syndrome was sitting on the floor, looking through a picture book. She looked familiar, but I didn't know where I had seen her. She wasn't in my class at Bristol Elementary. My parents went over to meet with the real estate agents, and I lagged behind. For some reason, I felt uncomfortable. My stomach tightened, but I didn't know why. *My Spider-Sense is tingling*, I thought. *Just like Spider-Man.*

As I sat on the floor near the entrance to the room, my parents chatted with John and Sarah Price. I glanced in their direction, and could only see the backs of my parents, sitting in chairs. John and Sarah were sitting opposite them, out of my view.

"Look at this," John said to my father. "It's a calculator. It can add numbers incredibly fast."

"And it's very accurate," added Sarah.

"It's amazing," her husband said.

"And it costs hundreds." Sarah's voice sounded concerned.

John glanced at Sarah. "But worth every penny."

"What will they think of next?" said my mother.

"So," said my father. "What would be a good house to start with?"

"There are tons of them," said John.

"But maybe you could suggest something specific to narrow it down?" asked my father.

"Well," said Sarah, "maybe the one on Chelsea Avenue." She looked at her husband.

"Yes," John said, the tone of his voice changing. "It would be a good starter house for you to buy and fix up."

"And it's on Chelsea?" asked my father.

"Yes," said John. "Do you know that area?"

"He knows all of Kansas City like the back of his hand," said my mother. "He used to be a driver for the fire department. Before he became a captain."

"Then you're interested in it?"

"Maybe," said my father. "We'll need to see it first."

"I'll take you over tomorrow," said John. "But if you want it, you'll need to move fast."

"Why's that?" asked my mother.

"Because it's only thirteen hundred dollars."

"How much did you say?"

"You heard me right." John nodded his head. "It's thirteen hundred dollars. But you'll need to move fast on it."

"We can go first thing tomorrow morning," said my mother. "Jack and Rebecca can come with us. They're good kids; they won't be any trouble."

"Rebecca is such a pretty name," said Sarah.

"Thank you," said Mom.

"I'd do anything to have a little girl like her."

"Then we have a plan," said John, and glanced at his wife.

"I think so, too," said Sarah. "Our daughter's name is Jenny." Her voice lowered. "She has special needs."

John stood up and my parents and Sarah stood as well. They shook hands and made small talk. They walked towards me, and I stood up.

"This is our son, Jack," said my mother.

"Nice to meet you," said John.

"You too," I said, looking up at him.

John looked to be about the same age as my oldest brother. He was tall, especially from the perspective of a five-year-old. He must have been over six feet, with piercing eyes, brown hair, and glasses. Sarah was much shorter. She had brown hair and also wore glasses. My eyes darted between John and Sarah. Suddenly, I realized why the little girl looked familiar. They were the three people from the car that keep circling our house that afternoon.

And my Spider-Sense was tingling.

2
BURIED SECRET

"That was them!" I said as soon as we stepped out of the Price's office.

"Shush!" said my father.

"Who?" asked my mother in a quiet voice as we moved away from the door.

"The people who were circling our house today."

"Harry," said my mother. "Jack said those were the people who were circling our house today."

"Not here," said my father. "Keep walking."

Mom and Dad talked about their new investment opportunity as we returned to our car. We climbed inside and began the drive home. The sun was setting as we made our way across town. My parents continued to talk about the good deal on the house, and their meeting with John the following day. They were excited at the possibility of an easy buy of a cheap house, and its earning potential for our family.

"I wonder why they were circling our house," I said.

"They were probably just curious about us," said Mom. "It's nice to know something about people you're doing business with. I can understand that."

"Besides," said my father. "Maybe it wasn't even them."

My mind flashed back to that afternoon. I was playing in our yard, and the car pulled up. The three inside—a man, a woman, and a child—turned and looked at me. And I thought of meeting John and Sarah in their office. I pulled the images together in my mind and knew they were the same people.

"It was them," I said as my father turned on the car's headlights. "I'm sure of it."

***

Sunlight shone through my bedroom window. As I opened my eyes to the early morning sunrise, dust particles floated in the beams of suspended light. They danced in the brightness, and the present moment and eternity touched.

A knock came at my door.

"Jack," came my mother's soft voice. "Time to get up. We have to go look at a house for sale."

My brown corduroy pants and blue-striped shirt lay on top of my dresser. The pants were a little short, as I was outgrowing them, but the shirt felt warm and comfortable. After dressing, I ran a comb through my hair and went downstairs for breakfast.

My mother was making bacon and scrambled eggs, along with buttered toast and a glass of fresh-squeezed orange juice. For some reason, I was nervous that morning. I didn't have much of an appetite and instead stirred my eggs with a fork.

"What's wrong, honey?" asked my mother. "Not hungry?"

"Not really," I smiled. "But it looks delicious."

"Try to eat a little," she said.

My little sister sat in the high chair next to me, eating her scrambled eggs. My mother wiped the baby's face and took off her bib.

My father came into the room, a big smile on his face. He winked at me.

"Good morning, little rascal."

"Good morning, Daddy."

"Ready to go on an adventure this morning?"

I perked up. I hadn't thought of today as an adventure.

"Yeah!"

We finished breakfast and loaded into our car. As we drove across Kansas City in the morning traffic, Mom and Dad chatted about the house we were going to look at. When we arrived, John Price was already there.

"Beautiful day," my father said as we climbed out of the family car.

"I'll take your word for it," said John. "Let's have a look-see at the house."

We walked up to the front door. The mailbox was packed with envelopes. John pulled out the mail and began leafing through it.

"Should you be doing that?" asked my mother, shifting my baby sister to her other hip.

John ignored her and continued to file through the envelopes. One caught his interest, and he opened it and began reading. He paused and looked up.

"It's fine," he said. "It's just the previous tenants' personal mail." He shrugged his shoulders. "They're gone."

My father and mother glanced at each other. After a moment, my father redirected him. "Let's go inside."

John put the letter and two other envelopes into his jacket pocket, and he put the rest back in the mailbox. He unlocked the door and we stepped inside.

The house had an old, musty smell. A faint scent of mold was in the air, and I could tell the previous owners had cats who weren't house-trained.

My parents began walking around the kitchen and dining room with John, and I explored the rest of the house on my own. The rooms were old and the paint was peeling, and there were brown stains on the walls. After touring through the main rooms, I went outside to play.

"Mom," I called into the other room. "Can I go outside?"

"Yes," said my mother. "Just be careful."

As I was leaving the front door, Mom said to John, "So, we will need to make a bid on the house?"

A gentle chill filled the air, an early sign Autumn would soon be upon us. As I walked through the high grass, I kicked my feet. Green weeds pushed through the broken sidewalk, drawing my attention to the ground. As I sat cross-legged on the concrete, I picked a dandelion puff. While twirling it in my fingers, I blew on it. My breath sent the seeds sailing through the air, like paratroopers leaping from an airplane. I stood and began searching the yard for more dandelions.

There were surprisingly few dandelions for such an overgrown lawn, and my quest soon led me to the side of the house. A perfect dandelion puff was waiting for me there. As I picked it, I imagined tiny fairies living in the flower. This time when I blew, I pictured the fairies flying off, being set free. Delighted, I continued hunting for more dandelions.

My search led me to the back of the house. There, several dandelions all stood in a row. I ran over and picked the first one. When I did, I noticed the plants were all in a line on one side of a board embedded in the ground. Dirt covered the board, but I could see the outline of a square. *Maybe it's a treasure chest.* I knocked on the board. It sounded like there was something under it.

As I knelt beside the board, I brushed off the soil. The board was nearly square and wedged into the ground. I dug my fingers into the soil along the edge of the board and tugged on it. It was firmly wedged in the dirt. Using both hands and pulling with all the strength my five-year-old body had, I lifted the board up.

A strong smell arose and I dropped the wooden board to the side. Waving the foul odor from my nose, I looked down to see what the board covered. There was a hole under where the board had been. But there wasn't a treasure inside. In the hole was the body of a decomposing woman. She was wrapped in a black plastic garbage bag, and her head hung down. The dead woman's knees were pressed up tightly to her chest, and her arms were pulled in close to her torso. I ran back to the house.

"Dad!" I yelled as I entered the house. "Dad, come quick!"

"Oh Jack," said my mother, shaking her head. "Your new white shoes are ruined."

"What's wrong?" my father asked.

"There's a woman outside!"

"What?" said my mother. "Where?"

"In the backyard," I said. "In a hole."

"In a hole?"

Yes," I said. "Mom, she's dead."

"Are you sure?"

"Yes," I said. My thoughts flowed back to the image of the decomposing body of the woman in the hole. "I'm sure."

"I wouldn't worry about it," said John. "It's probably really just a big dog."

"It wasn't a dog."

"Harry, go check it out," said my mother.

"I'm sure it's fine," my father said, putting his hand on my shoulder. "Probably nothing."

"Take us there," said my mother.

"Okay," I said. "This way."

As I walked to the door, I heard John say again, "Probably just a dog."

My parents and John followed me. Once we were outside, I looked for the dandelions marking the makeshift grave. The grass was low near the hole, and it was easy to find again.

"There it is," I said. "Over there."

"I don't see anything," said my mother.

"She's in a hole," I said. "Over there by the dandelions."

"Probably nothing," said John. "Let's look at the foundation of the house."

None of us moved.

After waiting a moment, I took a deep breath and walked towards the hole. This time I did not watch my white shoes moving through the tall grass. Dandelions held no interest for me. I was a man on a mission. As I walked, the sound of my parents' feet behind me brought some comfort. Dad was right, today was going to be an adventure. And if there was one thing I learned from comic books, it was that a hero had to follow an adventure through to the end. I kept walking.

"Probably nothing," I heard John call after us. "I wouldn't worry about it."

In a moment, I was back at the hole. Looking down into the hole, I saw the body again.

"There she is," I said, and pointed.

My father walked up next to me and looked in the hole.

"Mercy," he said, and made the sign of the cross.

"Oh my God," said my mother. "My God, she's dead."

For a moment, we stared in shock at the murdered woman.

"What are we supposed to do?" asked my mother.

"We need to tell someone," I said. "Someone who knows what to do."

"We have to contact the authorities," said my dad. "They'll take care of it."

John's shoes moved through the tall grass, swishing as he walked our way.

"I know how to handle it." John's voice came from behind us. "I'm a real estate agent. Not everyone can say that."

We stood in silence for a moment. In my mind, I prayed for the murdered woman and her loved ones.

"And I'm a bookkeeper," added John.

"You know what to do with a situation like this?" asked my mother.

"Of course," said John. "Like I said, I'm a professional. I'm highly trained. It's my responsibility."

"You'll call the police?" I asked.

"Well, maybe not the police," said John. "I think the Health Department is who we should contact."

"But someone murdered her," said my mother.

"We don't know that," said John. "It could be natural causes. Or just an unfortunate accident."

"She's wrapped in a garbage bag," replied my mother.

"And her body's been stuffed in a hole," I added.

"That's right, John," said my father. "Call the police."

"We don't want a dark cloud hanging over this house," said John. "You'll never get renters then."

"That's not important," said my father. "You need to call the police about it, John."

John was quiet and stared at the body. After a moment, he broke the silence.

"You're right. And don't worry, Sarah and I are friends with the police. I'll contact them and get this taken care of as quietly as possible."

"Do you need our help?" asked my mother.

"No," he said. "It's my responsibility as the real estate agent involved. Just take your kids and go."

"Thank you," said my father.

"Don't worry about a thing," John looked back towards the house. "I'll take care of it."

"You're sure?" said my mother.

"Of course," said John.

The wind picked up and the strange cool in the air became more noticeable. A chill ran through me. John looked at me and smiled.

"Trust me."

3
BEFORE THE NIGHT

As we drove back home, my parents talked about the murdered woman. They spoke in quiet voices, but little ears hear everything.

"I'm so glad John was with us," said my mother.

"Thank goodness for that," replied my father.

"How could a person murder someone in cold blood?"

"He must have been some kind of nut," said my father. "Only a crazy person would do something so horrible."

"Harry, we have to be careful," said my mother. "We're going to be visiting a lot of houses, and many of them are in the bad parts of Kansas City."

"It'll be fine," said my father. "Today was a once in a lifetime problem. Good to get it out of the way." He glanced at her and smiled.

"You're not afraid we'll stumble upon something like that again?"

"Impossible," said my dad. "Lightning never strikes twice."

Our gold 1965 Rambler Classic hit a bump, bouncing us hard. My father pulled to the side of the road and opened the door. He stepped out to check the tire.

"Can I come too, Dad?" I asked.

"Just wait here, Jack," said my mother. "He'll be right back."

"Mom, what happened to that lady today?"

"I don't know, Jack."

"Who killed her?"

"That's what the police will find out. They'll catch him and put him in jail."

"How will they catch him?"

"Oh, they use scientific methods today. No crime this serious will go unsolved for long. They'll probably arrest the killer in a few days. Don't be scared."

But I wasn't scared. Not one bit. I wanted answers. I didn't know things like this could happen. Until that day, I had lived in a world where both God and my parents were in complete control. Nothing could happen outside of their knowledge and their ability to stop it. I wanted a superhero to solve the problem and save the day. I wanted to *be* that hero. I wanted to be Superman.

"Mom, how could someone be so mean?"

"I wish I knew," said my mother. Mom turned around in her seat and looked at me. "Jack, don't tell your brothers about finding the body. I don't want to scare them."

I was disappointed. I wanted to tell my big brothers about what happened.

She was silent for a moment. "Hey, let's sing a song!"

"Okay!"

Mom began singing *Ragtime Cowboy Joe*. A smile spread across my face and soon I was clapping and singing along. After a few rounds, we came to the end of the song and both of us clapped with enthusiasm.

The car door opened and Dad sat down.

"Everything's fine," he said. "No harm done."

"They need to fix these roads," said my mother.

After a moment, she added, "So, you think we'll be safe?"

"Safe?" asked my father.

"You know," said my mother. Her voice lowered. "*Safe*. While we're house hunting."

"Absolutely," said my father. "There's nothing to worry about."

We turned onto a side street that always signaled to me we were almost home. My father glanced at my mother and smiled.

"And besides," he added, "John will be with us."

***

We arrived home and Mom made lunch—a grilled cheese sandwich and a bowl of tomato soup. I crumbled two saltine crackers into the steaming bowl of soup and watched them float on the crimson surface.

"So, what are you going to do today?" asked my father.

I shrugged my shoulders. "I don't know."

"It's a nice day to go for a walk," he suggested.

Nodding my head, I dipped my grilled cheese into the hot soup. "Maybe I'll walk around the neighborhood."

"Sounds like a good idea," said my mother. "Finish your lunch."

After I ate most of my grilled cheese and over half of the soup, Mom said I could go. I stepped out into the fresh air and walked over to the grapevine in our garden. The delicious scent of ripe grapes lingered in the air. Several plump pieces of fruit called to me. I picked one and popped it into my mouth. Moving it around with my tongue, I removed the skin. The sweet flavor of the grape filled my mouth. I left our garden and walked onto the street in front of our house.

The sunlight filtered through the branches of the nearby trees. The street was quiet and I walked downhill from our driveway. Before I knew it, I had circled the block. As I neared our driveway, my brothers Brad and Ed appeared over the hill. I ran to meet them.

"Hi guys," I said.

"Hey," said Brad.

"What've you been doing?"

"We went down to the train track," said Ed.

"Did you see any trains?"

"Yeah," said Ed. "Trains are really neat."

"What did you do today?" asked Brad.

"I went with mom and Dad to see a house."

"Oh yeah," said Ed. "And one train had spray paint all over it."

"Yeah," said Brad. "Kind of like art."

I nodded my head. I wanted to tell them about the murdered woman.

"What was the house like?"

"It was smelly."

"Old houses are shut up for a long time," said Brad. "They smell weird."

"Yeah," said Ed. "Was there a yard to play in?"

My thoughts flashed back to the body.

"Yes, but it wasn't fun to play in."

"Nothing to do there?"

"No," I said. "Not really."

"Is Dad going to buy it? asked Brad.

"I think so."

"Then we will be going over to fix it up," said Ed. "That'll be fun."

"I don't know how fun it will be."

"We'll make our own fun," said Brad.

"Come on," said Ed. "Let's play in the backyard."

Brad reached out and tapped me on the shoulder. "Tag! You're it!"

In a moment we were running after each other, laughing and playing. For a while, I forgot all about the house, the hole, and the murdered woman.

***

A few days later, life was back to normal. Dinner that night was steak and french fries. Mom peeled the potatoes and sliced them by hand. I loved to watch her melt the snow-white shortening, and then lower the raw potatoes into the hot oil. The taste was amazing and the memory of the hot fries still makes my mouth water. In those days, we didn't know about the dangers lurking in trans fat. We didn't know the dangers lurking anywhere. And ignorance was bliss.

"Harry," said my mother. "Would you like some iced tea?"

"Thank you," he answered. "This steak looks amazing."

My steak was about the size of my palm and cooked medium-well with mushrooms. When my mother sat down, I cut off a slice of the steak and took a bite. I poured my favorite vegetable, ketchup, onto my plate. Dipping a french-fry into the ketchup, I savored the moment with my family.

"Do you go back to work tomorrow, Dad?" asked Brad.

"That's right," he said. "I have to go back early this time. But I'm always as close as a phone call."

"Do you like being a firefighter?" asked Ed.

"I like it well enough," he said.

"I like the firetrucks," I said.

Brad and Ed both agreed at the same time.

Dad told us some stories about his past few days at work. I loved hearing about his adventures and my brothers and I sat rapt in awe. We ate together and laughed, and talked about the coming school year. When dinner was over, we took our plates to the kitchen and cleaned them off. Mom and Dad washed and dried them together, and we helped out in whatever small ways we could. When we had dried the last plate, we went into the living room to watch television. *All in the Family* was on, and we laughed at Archie Bunker and his family. *Scooby-Doo*, *Bugs Bunny*, and *Super Friends* were my favorites, but I loved watching anything with my family.

A knock came at the door. Mom answered it. She spoke for a moment to the person who knocked and then called to my father. Dad went to the door as my brothers and I continued to watch television. Over the sound of the laughter from the studio audience, I heard my father say, "Come in."

Glancing up, I recognized a now-familiar face.

It was John Price.

My memories from his visit are fuzzy. I was only five-years-old and exhausted from a hard day. Later in life, I asked my father for his memories of that night. I reconstructed the following from Dad's recollections.

John stepped inside our house and continued to talk with my parents. He was holding a bottle of cola in his hand. John's eyes scanned the room as he and my parents talked. I walked over to where they were standing. Mom and Dad were on my right and John was on my left. John looked down at me and spoke.

"Hi there, Jack."

"Hi."

"Here you go."

John reached out his hand and offered the bottle of soda to me. Wondering if it was okay to take it, I looked up at Dad.

"Can I have it, Dad?"

Dad smiled and nodded his head.

Excited, I took the cola bottle and said, "Thanks!"

The cap was already off, so I took a sip. I went into the living room to drink it. Mom and Dad finished their business with John. The door shut behind him as he left and my parents returned to watching television.

"What's that?" asked Brad.

"It's a cola," I said. I took a drink. "It's warm."

"Do we all get one?" asked Ed.

"I don't know," I said. "I don't think so."

"Lucky," said Ed.

Smiling, I took another sip.

"It tastes a little funny."

"Probably because it's an off-brand," said Dad.

My baby sister was watching me drink, so I got up and went into the dining room.

"Hey Jack, you're missing the show," my mother called.

"I know," I said.

"Can we make some popcorn?" Ed asked.

"That's a good idea," said my mother. "I'll go make some."

I sat at the dining room table and held my stomach. My mother passed by me on her way to the kitchen to make popcorn. Dad came in with her and stopped in the dining room. He noticed me sitting there and watched me for a moment.

"Are you okay?" asked Dad.

"I don't feel well."

"That's too bad," he said. "We're going to make popcorn. Want some?"

"No, thank you."

"No popcorn?" Dad replied and smiled. "You must be sick, it's one of your favorites."

Looking up at him, I managed a faint smile. Mom was in the kitchen working and the metal pot rang as she poured in the popcorn.

Dad watched me. "What do you feel like?"

"My legs are weak and I'm dizzy." I looked up at him. "And I've got a headache."

"If I give you a painkiller, will you take it?" He put his hand on my forehead to feel for a fever.

"What do you mean, a 'painkiller'?"

"You know," said my father. "A painkiller. Like aspirin or Tylenol. We just bought a new bottle today. If I give you one, will you take it?"

"Okay."

My father went into the kitchen and returned a moment later with a small white bag and a glass of water. He took the new medicine bottle out of the bag and easily popped the top off. He removed the cotton and poured two white pills into his hand.

"Here you go," he handed the two white painkillers and the glass of water to me.

Reaching out, I took the pills and glass of water in my hands. I held them in silence for a moment.

"You said you'd take it," he said.

Confused, I opened my hand and showed the painkillers to him. "I took it."

"No, Jack," said my father as he smiled. "Take it with some water and swallow it."

"No thank you," I said, handing them back to him.

"Okay," said Dad. He rubbed my hair with his hand. "Maybe you should go to bed early. You've had a long day."

I nodded my head. "Goodnight, Dad," I said, and climbed the stairs to my bedroom.

Although the first part of that evening is fuzzy, I remember the rest of that night very well. When I got to my room, I took off my shoes and pants; I was too sick to put on my pajamas. I climbed into bed and thought about the house on Chelsea, the hole, and the murdered woman. A funny taste lingered in my mind. My stomach cramped, and I tossed and turned in my bed. Something wasn't right. Nausea overcame me and I sat up in bed. Leaping up, I ran to the bathroom and began throwing up.

Dad was right. It had been a long day.

And I knew it was going to be a long night, too.

4
SHADOWS ON THE WALL

The moon was full that night. The pale light shone through my bedroom window as I held my stomach, too sick to sleep. My abdominal muscles ached from vomiting and I shook all over. Whenever I would cough, pain wracked my body. I knew Dad needed to sleep before returning to three days of work at the fire department, and I didn't want to wake him. Instead, I tiptoed downstairs to the guest room. That way I wouldn't wake him with my sickness.

The night seemed to last forever. I slid under the sheets in the guest bed, and the air in the room smelled stale from being unused for so long. I planned to wait until I heard the sounds of someone else awake, and then tell them I was sick. For hours, I rolled back and forth fitfully. At some point, I fell asleep and dreamed a series of repetitive dreams. In my dreams, we kept going to house after house. Every house we went to, there was a hole out back. Sometimes the hole was empty. Other times, it was filled with mud and water. And the lawns in my dreams were always high with grass and filled with dandelion puffs.

In the morning, I awoke to the sound of my mother's voice.

"Jack, are you all right?"

"I'm sick."

Mom came in and felt my forehead. She asked about my symptoms and I told her all that happened.

"We need to get you well before Monday," she said. "That's the first day of kindergarten."

Oh no, I thought. *I don't want to miss the first day of school.*

"I'll be okay."

"I'll get you some water," said my mother. "Don't worry, I'm sure you'll be fine."

As the day wore on, it was clear to my mother I wasn't fine. The long day passed into a second day. And then a third. My parents didn't believe in going to doctors unless there was a serious injury, and so I laid there in silence throughout the three days. I could sip a little water but I couldn't eat. By the fourth day, I hadn't gotten better. It was supposed to be the first day of school. My mother said I was too sick to go, and I felt disappointed.

"Don't worry," she told me. "You'll be better soon and you can start school then."

By the end of the first week, however, I was still too sick to start kindergarten. And at the end of the second week, my mother told me the sad news. She had called the school, and they told her I would be better off waiting until the next year to start kindergarten. Heartbroken, I laid alone in my room. To make matters worse, I was still very sick.

The days were boring and I missed playing with my friends. I passed the time watching the sunlight travel across my room, making shadows on the wall. When I was able, I read comic books. I knew Superman was invincible. *But even he has his Kryptonite*, I thought as I flipped through an old coverless comic for the hundredth time. The days and nights flowed together. At the end of the third week, a knock came at my bedroom door.

"Come in," I said.

The door opened and, to my surprise, John Price was standing there with my father.

"Jack," said my father. "John would like to talk to you."

"Okay."

John entered my room and kneeled by my bed. He put his elbows on my mattress, almost like he was praying. He looked at me for a moment, and then he spoke to my father without taking his eyes off me.

"I'd like to talk to Jack alone."

"Oh, okay," said my father. "Have a nice visit."

John waited as my father shut my bedroom door behind him and left. John looked me in the eye. I looked back and didn't blink. After a moment, he spoke.

"When did you first feel sick?"

"Three weeks ago."

"But exactly when?"

"I don't know."

"Try to remember," said John.

"It was the night you came to visit. After the ..." I was silent.

"After the house on Chelsea?"

"Yes," I said. "After I found the body." I thought for a moment. "Well, not right after."

"Then when?"

"After you left that night."

John nodded his head. "How long after that did you feel sick?"

"I don't know. We watched TV for a while. I went into the dining room. Then I felt sick."

"And you felt sick after I left?"

"I don't know, I guess so," I said. "I was sick, so I went to bed."

John nodded. "Do you feel better now?"

"Yes," I said. "I'm starting to feel better. But—"

"But what?"

"But it's too late to start school. I have to wait until next year."

"A lot of kids would love to have a year off school."

I shrugged my shoulders. "I guess. But I wanted to walk to school with my brothers."

John was silent and watched me without blinking. After a moment, he reached down and pulled up a long-handled flashlight. It was olive drab and looked huge to a five-year-old. John held it in his right hand and tapped it three times on his left palm. *Tap, tap, tap.* We both watched the flashlight drumming against his palm. He then tapped it three times again, this time firmly. *Smack, smack, smack.* John looked at me. Suddenly, he turned the flashlight around in his hand so that the handle was facing me.

"Here you go."

I glanced at the flashlight and then up at John.

"Take it," he said. "You can have it."

I reached out my hand and took it. *Wow,* I thought, *John Price is really nice.* John stood up and left my room without saying anything else. I held the flashlight in my hands and clicked it on. The light shone against my ceiling. Running my fingers in front of the light, I made shadows on the ceiling and walls. Rabbit ears bounced in the light, followed by a bird nipping at a bug, and then the Vulcan salute Spock always made on *Star Trek*. For the first time in days, I smiled.

"Wait till my brothers see this."

***

A few more days passed. The worst was over and I felt better. I was well enough to play outside, and early autumn was in the air. The neighborhood was quiet; most of the local kids were at school. Soon I was back to my old self, playing on our swing set, reading storybooks, and going for long walks in the neighborhood by myself.

One morning, I climbed up into our cherry tree. It was late in the season, so there were no cherries to be found. Reaching out, I plucked one of the dried stems left on a branch. Searching around on the barren limbs, I found a few more. My mother called to me. "Jack!"

Dropping a handful of dried stems, I scrambled down the tree and ran to our front porch.

"Hi, Mom."

"Hi," she looked at me and smiled. "Your father will be here in a minute and we are going to look at another house. Feel up for it? You can stay here alone if you prefer."

"I want to go, too," I said, glad to be going out. "Are we going alone?"

"No," said my mother. "John and Sarah will pick us up in their car. Go get ready."

I ran into the house and changed out of my play clothes. I put on a brown sweater and a pair of corduroy pants. As I combed my hair, I heard my father's voice downstairs. I ran down the stairs and straight into his arms for a hug.

"Looks like you're ready," he said with a smile.

"Can we wait outside?" I asked, excited about our day.

"Sounds like a good idea," he replied.

"I'll get my purse," said my mother.

Mom loaded a bag for the baby, and we all went outside into our yard. After a few moments, I saw John and Sarah pull up to the stop sign in front of our house. As they both turned and looked at us, I remembered the first time I saw them; they were in the same car and at the same stop sign. We hurried over and got in their car. The four of us sat in the backseat, and John and Sarah sat in front. John drove us across town to look at a house, and my mother and Sarah chatted as we drove.

"Sarah, where's your daughter, Jenny?" asked my mother.

"Jenny has a babysitter today," said Sarah. "It's hard to find someone who will babysit when your child has special needs."

"I'll bet," said my mother. "It must be so hard."

Sarah nodded. "I do the lady's taxes, and she watches Jenny when I need her to."

"She has to have another surgery," said John.

"Oh no," said my father.

"Yes, another heart surgery."

"She has heart problems, too?" asked my mother.

"Oh yes," said Sarah. "She's had surgery before. You never get used to it."

"Some people have kids so easily," said John. "It isn't fair."

"That's right," said my mother. "It isn't fair."

"*You* have kids very easy," said John. "Must be nice."

There was silence in the car for a moment. We were now in downtown Kansas City. John turned right onto a small side street.

"Kind of a scary neighborhood," said my mother.

"That's where you get the best deals on HUD houses," said Sarah.

"I'm sure you're right," said my father.

We turned right again, and I looked out of the car window at the rundown houses. We passed old chain-link fences, some of which were laying over on their sides. A yellow house had scorch marks on it where a fire had raged, destroying the upper left side of the home. After a few minutes of driving, our car came to a stop. Then I heard Sarah say, "Oh no."

"What's wrong?" said my mother.

"It's a street gang," said John. "They're blocking the road."

I leaned up and looked out the windshield. They were maybe a dozen men standing in front of our car. Their arms were covered with tattoos, and three of the men were not wearing shirts. One spit on the windshield in front of Sarah.

"Back the car up, John," said my mother. "We don't want any trouble."

"We can't," said John. "They're behind us, too."

I turned my head and looked out of our back window. Seven men stood behind our car, and one was holding a baseball bat. The man with the bat glared at me.

John honked the car horn.

"You honkin' at me?" shouted one man. Another man made an obscene gesture, and the rest crossed their arms and looked defiant."

"Turn left," said my father. "There is a side road there."

"I can't," said John.

"Go!" said my mother. "John, turn left. Now!"

"I can't!" shouted John.

"He can't turn left," said Sarah. "It's just something about him. He can't make left turns."

"What?" said my mother. "Why?"

"He just can't," said Sarah. "He has a lot of wonderful qualities, but making left turns isn't one of them."

"Get out of the car!" shouted one of the men.

"Get out of the car now!" shouted another.

"Maybe we better just do what he says," said Sarah.

My father glanced at my mother and then leaned up over the seat and grabbed the steering wheel. He turned the wheel hard to the left and shouted, "Hit the gas!"

John smashed his foot down on the accelerator. The tires screeched as the car shot to the left. As soon as we had made the left turn, John grabbed the wheel and my father sat back. We sped down the road and turned right onto the next street. We passed through two city blocks. John then pulled over on the right side of the road in front of a small white house.

"Here we are," said John, as if nothing had happened. "I'm sure you're going to love it."

"And the price is amazing," said Sarah.

John opened his car door and stepped out. He then opened my door and said to me, "You're going to love it, too."

John held my door open, and I got out of the car. As I looked up at the old white house, I heard John speak in a low voice, almost to himself.

"I know how much you like to explore backyards."

5
THE SHAPE OF THINGS TO COME

We decided not to buy the house, nor the next two houses we visited that morning. The next three weeks were quiet. We went house hunting a couple of times but found nothing of interest.

I spent my days walking the neighborhood and watching the autumn leaves change colors. When my brothers were home from school, we would sneak off to explore the train tracks. Sometimes we would find little makeshift shelters by the railroad tracks, where the homeless would sleep. They made the shelters with cardboard, scrap lumber, and anything else easily found in the area. My brothers and I would climb into them and look around. We never came across anyone living in one of the little shelters, but we would often find their belongings left behind.

When Brad was busy, my brother Ed and I would go exploring alone. One day we found a small shelter with a camp sink inside it. Ed pumped the handle on the sink, and water came out of the spigot.

"Wow," said Ed. "That's pretty cool."

"Yeah," I said and smiled. "Running water."

"I'd love to live in something like this," said Ed. "I'd fix it up with water, plumbing, and have some food."

I noticed a small bottle stuffed behind the sink. "What's that?"

Ed pulled the bottle out and we looked at it. It was half full with a brown liquid.

"What's inside the bottle?"

"I don't know," said Ed. He unscrewed the cap. "Tea?"

"Yeah, probably," said Ed. He took a sniff of the brown liquid. "Ugh." Ed turned his nose away from the bottle. "It must've gone bad. It stinks. Smell it." He held the bottle out to me.

"I believe you."

"Do you think we should pour it out?" asked Ed.

"Yeah," I said. "We don't want him to get sick."

Ed nodded and poured the foul-smelling liquid down the drain of the camp sink.

In the distance, the sound of a train whistle echoed throughout the valley.

"Let's go," I said.

Ed and I crawled out and began our long walk back home. As we walked, I wondered if I should tell him about the murdered woman I had found.

"Ed?"

"Yeah?"

"Have you ever found anything weird at the train tracks?"

"What do you mean?"

"You know, something strange. Something you should tell the police about."

"You mean like the hobo houses?"

"No," I said. There was a crushed Coke can in the road and I kicked it. "Something bigger than that."

"Like pirates' treasure?"

"Yeah, something like that."

"I wouldn't tell anyone if I found pirates' treasure. I'd rebury it somewhere else and draw a map to it."

I smiled. "With an 'X' marking the spot where they buried the treasure."

"Yeah," he agreed.

I took a deep breath. "But what if the pirates came after you?"

"You mean to get their treasure back?"

"Yeah," I said. "Or maybe to cover up their crime."

"What crime?"

"Well, I've always assumed the pirates stole the treasure. What if they didn't want to get caught? If they knew you had found the treasure, they would come after you, right?"

"Right."

"So, what would you do?"

Ed shrugged his shoulders. "I guess I'd keep it a secret. I wouldn't tell anyone."

"Not even me?"

"Not even you."

"How about Mom and Dad?"

Ed shook his head. "Because if the pirates came after me, Mom and Dad would be in danger, too. And so would you. But what you don't know can't hurt you."

"I don't think that's true."

Ed shrugged. "That's what they say."

We caught up to the crushed can I had kicked a moment before. This time Ed kicked it and it sprang several feet in front of us, scraping the road as it bounced along.

"Besides," Ed continued. "The pirates wouldn't know it was me who found the treasure."

"What if they saw you find it?"

"They wouldn't."

"What if they were someone you knew?"

"Like who?"

"I don't know. Maybe a friend of Mom and Dad."

"I wish they knew some pirates," said Ed. "That would be neat."

"Well, maybe not pirates. I don't think there are any these days. But maybe some other kind of criminal."

It was my turn to kick the can. It sailed 10 feet in front of us.

"Nice kick," said Ed.

"Thanks," I said, and smiled.

"I can't imagine anyone Mom and Dad know who might be criminals."

I shrugged my shoulders. "Maybe John and Sarah."

"Oh, they aren't criminals."

"But just pretend for a moment. What if they were criminals, and they knew you could connect them to a crime? What would be the right thing to do?"

Ed shrugged his shoulders. "It would have to be a pretty serious crime."

"Pretend it was."

"Like what?"

"Well, what if it was murder?"

"Who would John murder?"

"Just pretend."

"Well, I guess I would tell Mom and Dad after all. They would know what to do."

"That's all you would do?"

We came again to the crushed tin can in the road.

"Jack," said Ed. "We're just kids. That's all we could do."

The crushed soda can lay at my feet. I gave it a hard kick. The wind caught the flattened can and it sailed off towards the ditch. For a moment, the sunlight reflected off the aluminum; the shiny metal flashed in the autumn air. Then it flew into the brush and it was gone.

"I guess you're right," I said. "But somehow, it doesn't seem enough."

***

The following Monday morning, my parents took me and my baby sister to a meeting with John and Sarah. When we got to their office, my stomach tightened. *My spider-sense is tingling.* Their office smelled of stale macaroni and cheese. My parents had explained to me earlier that the Prices were living in the office, and Sarah would cook a week's worth of food at a time. They would eat the food throughout the week and restock after that. As we entered their office, I saw their daughter Jenny looking out the window at the street below.

"Hi Jenny," said my mother. "What are you doing?"

"She likes to look out of the window and wave at the people below," said Sarah. "Sometimes they wave back. Jenny likes that."

My mother walked over to Jenny and patted her on her back. "It's fun to look out at people."

"Jack," said my mother. "Come, take a look."

John looked at me as I walked over to the window. Looking out at the street below, I saw a man coming in our direction. Jenny waved at the man and he smiled and waved back. Jenny giggled and clapped her hands.

"He waved back," I said to my mother.

Sarah walked over to the window and looked out.

"Oh, that's Raymond West," said Sarah. "He always waves to Jenny."

"That's nice," said my mother.

"Yes," said Sarah. "And we made a business connection with him. We do his taxes."

"He's got a lot of money for a working man," said John.

"Oh?" said my mother.

"Yeah, well, he works and doesn't have many expenses," said John. "He lives in his mother's little house a few blocks away."

"Does he have a wife and kids?" asked my father.

"No," said Sarah. "He's not married."

"Is your oldest son Darren married?" asked John.

"No," said my mother. "He's divorced."

"That's too bad," said Sarah.

"Did Darren go to Vietnam?" John asked.

"No," said my father. "He wasn't drafted and he didn't join." He paused a moment and then added, "He believes in nonviolence."

"Thank goodness they didn't draft him," said my mother. "We were afraid he'd have to go. He's too sensitive. It would have killed him."

"He was in college," my father added. "So, he was exempt from the draft."

John snapped his fingers. "I just remembered; I have some papers for you to sign."

"Okay," said my father.

Dad and John went to a desk. John had a file opened and they sat together. They discussed business while my mother and Sarah continued their conversation.

Mom and Sarah spoke quietly. Their voices never rose above a whisper. Although I couldn't hear it at the time, Mom told me about her conversations with Sarah years later. This one went something like this:

"Was John drafted?" my mother asked.

"No," said Sarah. She glanced at John and lowered her voice. "John's background prevents him from military service."

"Why is that?"

"Well, let's just say he had a tough upbringing."

"I'm sorry to hear that," said my mother.

Sarah was quiet for a moment. Then she continued whispering. "They admitted him to a mental hospital."

"A crazy house?" asked my mother.

"Shh!" said Sarah, glancing at John. "No, no, just a psychiatric facility."

"Oh," said my mother. "That's too bad." She paused a moment, and then asked, "What happened?"

"Well, they diagnosed him with catatonic schizophrenia."

"That sounds serious."

Sarah nodded. "He was raised by foster parents. Witnesses claim they saw him chasing his foster mom with an ax, and they freaked out." She shook her head. "Some people."

"Oh my," said my mother.

"Don't worry," said Sarah. "He was just a teenager, and they always do crazy stuff like that. Right?"

"Well," said my mother. "I suppose."

"Besides," added Sarah, "he had treatment. He got better and they released him. That's where I met him. John and I always tell people we met in college. But the mental hospital is where we really met."

"You were in the crazy hou …" Mom paused. "The *psychiatric facility*, too?"

"No," said Sarah. "I volunteered at the little library there. John would come in and sit for hours. We'd talk. He was the first guy who liked me. Growing up, everyone liked my sister better. She got the looks, but I got the brains."

"Brains are better, anyway." My mother smiled at Sarah.

"That's what I think," Sarah smiled back.

"So that's what John did to get sent for treatment?" asked my mother. "He chased his mother with an ax?"

"Yes, just the ax thing. That's all." Sarah paused. "Well, that and the thing with his father."

"What happened with his father?"

"Oh, nothing really. They got into a fight, and John beat him up pretty bad. No big deal. Boys will be boys. Right?"

"I'm glad he's better now."

"Yes, and he felt a lot of remorse for everything that happened." Sarah paused. "I think so, anyway. John may not admit it, but I'm sure he feels bad about it. He even tried to commit suicide."

"He did?"

"Yes," she said. "He took 36 painkillers."

"What kind of painkillers?"

Sarah shrugged. "Some kind of headache tablets."

"He did that because he felt bad about what he did to his parents?"

"Uh-huh." Sarah paused. "Well, I guess so. That, and to get out of being drafted."

"Oh my," said my mother. Her forehead wrinkled, but she said nothing.

Sarah stared back at my mother in silence and didn't blink. After an uncomfortable moment, she said, "Mrs. Kerrigan, I shouldn't have told you all that. John would be furious if he knew I had told you. I feel you're a friend. Someone I can talk to. Someone I can trust. Please don't tell Mr. Kerrigan what I said about John."

"I won't," said my mother. "I understand completely."

Sarah looked relieved. "Thank you so much." Sarah paused. "And Mrs. Kerrigan, please don't tell John either."

"It will be our little secret," whispered Mom.

Sarah smiled at my mother.

Mom glanced at me and spoke up in a loud voice. "Jack, go play so Sarah and I can chat."

I nodded. "Okay."

My eyes scanned the office for something fun to do. My mother was looking hard at me, and I knew I should leave the window area. As I was walking away, I heard my mother say, "Tell me more about John's background ..."

As my mother and Sarah talked, I noticed a small bookshelf against the wall. Books always fascinated me, so I perused their collection. Coloring books, children's stories, and tax guides filled the shelves. One book grabbed my attention. I pulled it out and looked at the cover.

"We're going to look at a house." My father's voice startled me, and I raised my eyes from gazing at the cover of the book.

"Okay," I said and put the book back.

"You're probably getting bored."

"No, I'm fine."

My father smiled and patted my shoulder. "I haven't forgotten what it's like to be a kid," he said. "We'll drop you off at Saint Francis House, and you can spend some time with your brother Darren. Would you like that?"

"Yeah!"

My father laughed. "Great, we'll keep the baby with us, so you can have some time without having to watch her."

As I went and stood by the door, my father pulled a large book from the bottom shelf and looked at it. The smile faded from his face as he read the cover. He thumbed through the pages; his face was serious. Mom and Sarah finished their conversation, and Mom walked over to my father.

"What's that book about?"

Dad looked my mother in the eye and quietly said only two words.

"Potassium cyanide."

6
THE SINS OF CYANIDE

As we drove through the busy traffic of Kansas City, Mom talked about John and Sarah's daughter, Jenny.

"Poor child," said my mother. "She's already had five heart surgeries."

"I can't imagine how hard that must be," said my father.

"I know," said Mom. "And all that on top of having Downs Syndrome."

"So sad," said my father. "Some people have so much to deal with."

Mom nodded her head. "And the poor girl hasn't recovered well from the last surgery."

"I hope she'll be all right."

"Me too," said my mother. She shook her head. "If anything happened to that little girl, I'm worried about what it would do to them."

We rode in silence, the hum of the engine and the growl of the tires on the road the only sound. After a few minutes, Mom broke the hypnosis of riding through traffic.

"Tell me more about the book you found in John and Sarah's office."

Dad glanced over at Mom. "It was about how to make booby-traps, grenades, bombs, poisons. Stuff like that."

"Oh my," said Mom.

Dad nodded. "It showed how they could be made cheaply out of everyday materials."

"I wonder why he would have a book about all that," said Mom.

"I don't know," he said. "It also said you could put rhubarb leaves in a salad or on a sandwich and kill someone."

"Rhubarb leaves?"

"Yeah, Rhubarb leaves are poison," said Dad, "but the book said they look like a normal thing to eat."

"That's horrible," said Mom.

Dad nodded and went on telling her about the odd book. "It even advised readers to test the poisons by leaving tainted bottles in 'wino nests.'"

"Sickening."

"I know," said Dad. "The book said if you find a dead body in it the next morning, you've figured out the correct dose."

As Dad spoke, I remembered the makeshift shelter down by the train tracks. The bottle of brown liquid with its foul smell came to mind. *I hope someone didn't poison that guy.*

Dad continued. "There were designs and drawings of various bombs, guns, and weapons in the book," he said. "On the side of the front cover was a list of some of the how-to articles inside."

Dad turned on the blinker and passed the slow-moving car in front of us. After a moment, he went on describing the book.

"The title of one article jumped out at me," he said.

"The one about cyanide poison?" asked Mom.

My father nodded.

"Dad?"

"Yes?"

"What's cyanide?"

There was a long pause.

"Cyanide?" said my mother. "Why do you want to know about that?"

"I don't know." I shrugged my shoulders. "Dad saw it in John's book, right?"

Mom glanced at Dad and whispered, "Oops."

"Well, it was just a book of information," said my father. "That's all. I wouldn't worry about it."

"I'm not worried," I said.

There was a long silence.

"So, what's cyanide?"

"It's a poison," said my father. "They say it smells like burnt almonds. It kills fast in high-enough doses, but small amounts of it are found in nature."

"It smells like burnt almonds?"

"That's what they say," said my father.

"It's in rat poison, I think," said my mother.

"I don't think it's in rat poison, but it's pretty common," said my father. "It *is* used to kill pests, though. You know, a pesticide."

"So," said my mother, "basically, rat poison."

My father shrugged his shoulders and nodded. "There's a small amount of it in cigarette smoke," he said, "but it's toxic in the right dosage."

"Could it be used to kill people, too?"

"Oh yes," said my father. "They used it in World War I."

"Amazing how people can find more and more ways to kill each other," said my mother.

"Yeah," I said.

"Also," said my father, "some of the Nazis used it to commit suicide at the end of World War II."

My father served in World War II, and he had done a lot of reading about the war since. He wasn't in combat, but he still knew a lot about famous historical figures and battles of the war. Dad served in the Coast Guard on horse patrol in California. He and his fellow guardsmen would ride up and down the beach and scout for Japanese submarines. Dad loved history and could talk at length about the war. I loved hearing stories about his time in the Coast Guard. My father was even friends with Alan Hale, Jr., famous for playing the Skipper on the television show *Gilligan's Island*. And to a five-year-old boy, that was just about as cool as you could get.

"Like who?" I asked.

"Oh, Eva Braun, Goebbels, people like that. Goebbels even had cyanide administered to his six young children."

"Harry," said my mother.

"Oh, and Hitler killed himself with it, too. He took it and then he shot—"

"Harry!"

"Hmm?"

"There's *Saint Francis House* on the left, dear."

We pulled into the driveway of the old house where my brother lived. It was a community house with both men and women living there. They wanted to live simply and peacefully in the way of Saint Francis, but they weren't part of a religious order. He and his friends shared their expenses and household chores. The spiritual community ate meals together and had interesting discussions. Darren met us as we were getting out of the car. He had a long beard and a big smile spread across his face. He was wearing brown shoes, a navy-blue t-shirt, and Levi jeans.

"Darren!" I ran and hugged my big brother.

"Hi Jack," said Darren. "Want to hang out for an hour or so?"

"Yeah!"

Darren chatted with our parents for a few minutes, and then he and I went inside *Saint Francis House*. The house smelled like homemade bread and fresh-baked cookies. There were two men and one woman in the living room. The woman and one man sat on an old green couch. The other man sat in a wicker chair. In the center of the room was a brown coffee table, and on the table was a wood carving of two hands pressed together. Next to the sculpture was a well-worn leather Bible; a set of black rosary beads rested on the cover. The dark wood of the sculpture intrigued me. I ran my fingers over the smooth wood. The gentle scent of linseed oil lingered in the air.

"Do you like that?" asked the woman. She had long, straight, brown hair. She wore a simple jean dress over a white shirt. A wooden cross hung from her neck, and she had round-rimmed glasses.

"Yes, I like it," I said. "It's so smooth."

"My brother made it." The woman smiled. "I'm Mary Catherine."

"Nice to meet you," I said. "I'm Jack."

"Nice to meet you, too, Jack."

"I'm Richard," said a tall man with a big smile. His brown hair was almost as long as Mary Catherine's, and his beard was about the same length as my brother's beard. He was sitting on the couch next to Mary Catherine.

"Hi," I said.

"Jack's going to stay here for about an hour," said my brother. He then turned to me and said, "Will you be okay here for a few minutes?"

I nodded my head, and Darren left the room. I ran my fingers over the sculpture again. After a moment, Mary Catherine spoke.

"Do you have any questions about this place, Jack?"

"Not really. What do you do here?"

"It's a pretty normal house. We pray, take turns making meals, stuff like that."

"Jack looks like the kind of guy who has bigger questions than that," said Richard, smiling.

"When I was a boy," said the other man, "I always wished I could ask questions about important things, but I never felt I could. If you could ask any question, Jack, what would it be?"

I thought for a moment. "Why is there badness in the world?"

The man leaned forward in the wicker chair. "What do you mean?" he asked. He wore a white t-shirt with a silver cross dangling from a chain. His hair was cut short and parted to the right, and his beard was well-trimmed.

"I know God is good and strong," I said. "So, why is there so much badness?"

"We have a theologian here," said Mary Catherine.

"Well, that *is* a big question," said the man. "My name is Anthony, by the way."

"Hi, Anthony."

"Evil doesn't exist," said Anthony. "Not in and of itself, anyway. Evil is just the absence of good. Like darkness is the absence of light."

"I don't know about that," said Mary Catherine. She turned to me, her warm smile lighting up the room. "It's complicated, Jack. There is a plan, but we can't understand it. At least, not yet."

"Do you have a specific 'badness' in mind?" asked Richard.

"I don't know," I said. "Let's say ... *murder*."

"Murder!" said Mary Catherine. "Okay, guys, time to change the subject. Jack, I made fresh cookies and they should be barely cool enough to eat. Would you like one?"

"Yeah!"

"Great!" said Mary Catherine, her eyes twinkling. "And we have some farm-fresh milk, too. Ice cold!"

Mary Catherine took my hand and led me towards the kitchen. As we were leaving the room, Richard said my name. Turning back, I looked at him. His face was kind but serious.

"God has a right hand and a left hand," he said. "And both do his will."

"Enough deep thoughts," said Mary Catherine, and ushered me into the kitchen.

The kitchen smelled of natural gas and fresh-baked cookies. She poured a glass of milk and offered me a seat at a wooden table. Mary Catherine used a spatula to lift two cookies from the baking sheet to a plate. She set the plate in front of me, along with the milk. Mary Catherine sat in the chair beside me.

The voice of my brother, Darren, came from the hallway. Looking in his direction, I saw Darren talking to a huge man. The large man wore a red t-shirt and brown slacks. He had dark, messy hair and a patchy beard.

"I don't know," said Darren. "I only know they've bought several houses and hope to retire soon."

"So, your folks have a lot of money?" asked the heavy-set man.

"Like I said, I don't know. I don't think so. Dad's just a fire captain."

"But he's going to retire early," said the man. "That takes money."

"Well, yeah," said Darren. "That's why they buy old houses and fix them up. They re-sell them or rent them to make extra money."

"It takes money to make money," said the man.

"I guess," said Darren.

"Where are they going to live when they retire?" asked the man.

Darren shrugged his shoulders. "They want to move out of Kansas City."

"To the country?"

"Yes," said Darren. "They'd like to have a country farm and raise the kids out there."

"Out where?"

"Oh, I don't know. Somewhere in the country."

There was a long pause. "Yeah, but *exactly* where?"

"I don't know," said Darren. He glanced at me. "I need to go; my little brother is here."

The man looked at me. "That's your little brother?"

"Yeah," said Darren. "I have three little brothers and one little sister. She's just a baby."

"Very interesting," said the man. "Why is your brother here? Is he going to be living here?"

"No," said Darren. "I'm just watching him for a little while."

"Do your parents need a babysitter?"

"Sometimes, I guess," said Darren.

"I'd be happy to do that for them," said the man. "No charge."

"I'll keep it in mind," said Darren. "Look, I need to go."

The heavy-set man nodded his head, glanced at me, and then left. Darren walked over to the table and smiled at me.

"Who's that?" I asked.

"Oh," said Darren. "That was Tracy."

"Does he live here?"

"No," said Darren. "We keep an open house, and he comes in sometimes. That's all."

"He's not a member here?"

"No," said Darren.

"Oh," I said. "Is he your friend?"

"Not really," he said. "He just comes in sometimes and talks. We believe all are welcome. All means all."

"How does he know about Mom and Dad? Or about our houses?"

"He's a friend of John and Sarah Price. He says he works for them. Tracy is the guy who gave me John's name and number. That's how Mom and Dad met them."

"Oh, okay." I dipped a cookie into the milk. "So, he's a nice guy?"

Darren looked at Mary Catherine. For a moment, neither of them spoke. Then Darren broke the silence.

"Eat your cookies," he said. "Mom and Dad will be here to take you home any minute."

Pulling my cookie out of the milk, I looked at it. "What flavor are they?" I asked.

"Almond," said Mary Catherine.

I put the cookie back on the plate.

7
CHILDREN OF BLOOD

The next few weeks were uneventful. The weather turned cold and early winter replaced the cool autumn air. My father's job at the fire department came with certain fringe benefits, not the least of which were free movie tickets. And so, some evenings we would go to the *Englewood Theater* in Independence, and watch movies together. Dad would show his badge and the owners would let us in. The smell of hot-buttered popcorn and the excitement of a darkening theater marked 1974. That year we went to see *Young Frankenstein*, *The Towering Inferno*, and the James Bond movie, *The Man with the Golden Gun*. Other than that, we spent our free time fixing up the houses we had bought. We would paint them, repair a few broken things, and mow the lawns. We then would either resell them or rent them to tenants.

My father continued his work pattern of three days on at the fire department, followed by three days off. Sometimes I would spend a few hours with him there while my mother ran errands. I loved talking with the firefighters and playing with the firehouse dog, a friendly dalmatian with white fur and black spots. I would sit on the cool cement floor and pet him, and he would roll over on his back and invite me to scratch his belly. But I especially loved climbing on the firetrucks and sliding down the fire poles. Dad kept a bag of caramels in his office for when I would visit. Ever since then, the sound of unwrapping a caramel and the sweet taste of the candy brings back those magical days with my father.

One day after he got off work, my father drove me to pick up my mother and baby sister from an appointment. John Price had told my father about a small property auction where we might find some good prices on foreclosed houses. John and Sarah couldn't go; their daughter Jenny was not recovering well from her last heart surgery. She was in a lot of pain and very sick. But my parents wanted to check the auction out anyway.

"This is exciting," said my father as we drove through Kansas City. "I've never been to an auction before."

"I wonder if it's like in the movies," I said.

"Like what?" asked my mother.

"You know," I said. "Auctioneer talk. 'Five-dollar bid, five-dollar bid, and ten. Ten, ten, ten. Do I hear twenty?' Stuff like that."

Mom and Dad broke out laughing.

"That's pretty good, Jack," said my mother. "Maybe you'll be an auctioneer one day."

"Or an actor," said my father, and he glanced at me in the rearview mirror and smiled.

The traffic in front of us came to a stop. We slowed down and then stopped behind the car in front of us. In front of that car was a police car. As we sat in silence at the stoplight, I looked at the lights on the roof of the police car.

"Do it again," said my mother.

"What?" I said.

"The auctioneer thing, do it again."

"Ten, ten, ten," I said, smiling. "We got ten. Do I hear twenty? Come on folks, do I hear—"

Just then, a car traveling at full speed crashed into the rear of our Rambler. The impact sent me flying forward into the back of the driver's seat. My body smashed into the seat, saving me from going through the windshield. Mom's head struck the dash in front of her hard and my father's head hit the steering wheel. My baby sister flew into the back of the passenger seat, crashed against it, and crumpled to the floor. Her crying filled the car, and I reached out to comfort her. The red light changed to green and traffic moved forward. Dad honked the horn several times to get the attention of the police. They didn't respond. Then Dad jumped out of the car, waved his arms, and yelled for the police officer to help. Pulling myself up, I looked out the windshield at the police car. The officer looked at my father in his review mirror and then drove away.

Several good citizens stopped to help us, and the woman who hit us came running up crying.

"Oh my God!" she screamed. "I hurt the baby! I hurt the baby!"

"It's okay," said my father, trying to comfort her. "Don't worry, it's okay."

"Harry," said my mother. "It's *not* okay. She hit us!"

"Ma'am, I'm so sorry," said the woman. "Is the baby okay?"

"I think she's okay," said my mother. "But we need to call the police."

"I'm so sorry," said the woman. "Oh my God, I hope I didn't hurt the baby!"

In twenty minutes, the police were there. They wrote an accident report and issued the lady who hit us a ticket. The property auction was only a block away, so after the police were finished, we drove to the parking lot at the auction. We got out of the car and I went to look at the damage. The rear lights were smashed out and the trunk was crumpled, but it was still drivable. My mother held the baby close and we all stood in silence.

After a few moments, my father spoke.

"We're going to skip the auction and go back home," he said. "But we needed to rest a few minutes first. Betty, how is Rebecca?"

"I think she's okay," she said. "Just scared."

A voice came from behind us. "Hi there."

We turned and looked. A tall, heavyset man wearing an orange shirt and black pants was walking towards us. He was smiling, but in a strange forced sort of way. I recognized him at once as the man named "Tracy" who was at *Saint Francis House* a few weeks ago.

"Hi," said my mother.

"How you folks doing?"

"Not so good," said my mother. "We were just in a car accident."

"Sorry to hear that," said the man.

My father leaned his head down and whispered, "Don't talk to strangers in parking lots."

Tracy walked over to look at the rear of our car.

"They really did a number on you," he said. "Smashed you up terribly."

We were silent for a moment.

Tracy looked at us. "I'm a friend of John and Sarah Price." He paused. "Oh, and I know your son, Darren. I was the one who gave him John and Sarah's number to give to you."

"Oh, that's good to know," said my mother. "You can't be too careful these days."

"Ain't that the truth?" said Tracy. He paused and looked at the baby. "This is Rebecca, right?"

"Right," said my mother. "How do you know her name?"

"Sarah Price told me all about her," he said. "Let me hold her for you."

"That's okay," said my father.

Tracy walked over and began petting the baby. "Come on," he said. "Let me hold her a while." He paused and then added, "I won't bite."

"No thank you," said my mother.

"I'll just take her on a little walk around the neighborhood," Tracy said. "Just to help you folks out a little. That's all."

"No thank you," said my father.

"Here," said Tracy, reaching out to take her. "We'll be right back. Won't we—"

"No!" said my mother.

"I think you had better leave," said my father. "Now."

Tracy looked at us without blinking. My father looked back at him the same way. After a moment, Tracy said, "No problem, no problem, I'm just trying to help you folks out. That's all."

Tracy turned to leave. He took a few steps and then stopped. He turned back and looked at us.

"By the way," he said. "Are them boys of yours home alone?"

***

That evening, Mom made fried chicken and homemade mashed potatoes for dinner. We had buttered corn and sliced tomatoes as side dishes. For dessert, Mom made cherry tarts with white icing. After dinner, we sat in the living room. Mom made a pot of coffee for her and Dad, and the rest of us sipped iced tea as we talked about our day.

"There should be a law requiring seatbelts," my mother said as she sipped her coffee. "We were lucky no one was hurt today."

"We don't need another law," said my father. "You need to have a lawyer just to leave the house as it is."

"Did the police arrest the lady who hit you?" asked Brad.

"No," said my father. "Just a ticket. She admitted fault."

"Harry," said my mother. "I wonder how that man knew we would be at the auction. John was the only one who knew we were there. Even Darren didn't know."

"John must have told him," said Dad.

"But I wonder why," said my mother. "And I didn't like that he knew so much about us."

My father shrugged. "Some people are just a little weird, that's all."

"By the way," said my mother to my brothers and me. "If you are ever here alone, don't answer the door if someone knocks."

"Okay," said Brad.

"We'll only let them in if they say they know you," said Ed.

"No," said my mother. "Don't let them in, even if they say they know us."

"Remember," said my father, "just because someone knocks, it doesn't mean you have to answer."

"And sometimes you shouldn't," said my mother.

"What if it's Darren?" asked Ed.

"Darren's fine," said my mother.

"How about John and Sarah Price?"

"Oh, I'm sure they're fine," said my father. "But not strangers." He glanced at my mother. "No use scaring them too much. I think they get the message."

"Yes, I agree," said my mother.

"What did you two do today?" my father asked my brothers.

"We went down to the post office," said Ed.

"What for?" asked my mother.

"To look at pictures of criminals," said Brad.

"I wish I could have gone," I said. "That sounds fun."

"It wasn't," said Ed.

"Yeah," said Brad. "You can't take the pictures with you. You just have to look at them there."

"That's weird," I said. "How can you catch a criminal without a picture?"

"I know, right?" said Brad.

The telephone rang, and my mother went to answer it.

"You don't need to worry about catching criminals," said my father. "That's what the police are for."

The image of the police officer driving away from the accident scene today came to my mind. *Maybe he was going to catch a criminal,* I thought. *Maybe he was in a hurry to catch whoever murdered the woman I found in the hole.*

"Yeah," I said. "But sometimes they need our help."

My mother was still talking on the phone. It sounded like she was crying. I got up and went into the dining room to check on her. As I was leaving the living room, I heard Brad saying, "Maybe if we go back, we could get some of the pictures and take them with us ..."

"Oh John, that's so sad," said my mother. Tears were running down her face. "I'm so sorry." She was quiet as she listened for a few minutes. She started sobbing. "Do you know when the funeral will be?" She listened for a moment. "Oh John, please don't do that. Don't donate her body to science. You need to have a funeral. You need closure."

My mother looked at me and tried to smile through the tears. I went into the guest room to give her some privacy. After a few moments, she came in.

"Jack," my mother said, her eyes red and her face wet with tears. "Don't be afraid. Something sad happened, that's all. It's natural to cry when something sad happens."

"What happened?" I asked.

"John and Sarah's little girl, Jenny," she said. She stopped speaking and looked down for a moment. "She died." Mom started sobbing again.

"I'm sorry, Mom," I hugged her. "Don't cry."

"It's okay for people to see you cry, Jack. People don't care if you see them angry, but they don't want you to see them cry. It should be the other way around."

"How'd she die?"

"Her last surgery went bad."

"I know," I said. "But that was a few weeks ago."

"She never got better. She was in a lot of pain. They called a doctor, and he told them to give her a painkiller."

"Did they give it to her?"

"Yes, but she got worse and worse. They had to rush her to the hospital." Mom paused. She furrowed her brow. "But she didn't make it. A blood vessel near her heart ruptured."

Mom walked over and looked out the window. For a few minutes, she said nothing. After a long silence, she looked back at me. She came over and hugged me tight. Her tears rained down upon my head and my hair became wet.

"Little Jenny died in John's arms," she said. "And there was nothing he could do to stop it."

8
HIDE AND SEEK

Winter passed into spring, and spring faded into summer. In August, I turned six years old, and I was ready to take on the world. My brothers and I spent the hot weather playing in our neighborhood. We walked around town, played basketball, and went to the train tracks. Sometimes we would walk to a nearby grocery store and bring home bread and milk. And each afternoon, the ice cream truck would drive by playing its haunting melody. When we had enough spare change, we would run out, flag down the driver, and buy ice cream.

Kindergarten at Bristol Elementary started towards the end of summer, and I was excited to begin. My mother had taught me how to read when I was four years old, and my teacher noticed right away that I was an excellent reader. She arranged for me to do my reading time with the 3rd Grade class. Every day during story time, a young woman named Trish would come to my kindergarten class and get me. She would walk me to the 3rd Grade class so I could join them for their reading time. And as we walked, we would talk.

"How was your summer?" she asked me one Friday morning. Trish had long blond hair and was dressed in bellbottom jeans, brown boots, and a paisley blouse.

"It was great."

"Anything fun happen?"

"Yeah, I played with my brothers and little sister. We went to the park. Stuff like that."

"I hear you're a good reader."

"I guess so."

"Do you like books?"

"I love them. I like to go to the library with my parents."

"You're six years old?"

"Yeah," I said. For some reason, I felt the need to explain why I was in kindergarten. "I was sick last fall and couldn't start school on time."

Trish nodded. "That's too bad," she said. "What made you so sick?"

My mind flashed to all happened in the past year—the murdered body I had found, the cola bottle, and the terrible sickness.

I shrugged my shoulders. "I don't know, I just got sick."

I started to tell her about Jenny dying and how Mom said John had changed so much since then.

But I didn't. I just kept walking with her to the 3rd Grade class.

After we got to the classroom door, Trish looked at me and smiled.

"You're a neat guy, Jack. I like you."

Smiling back, I went in and read with the older kids.

After reading, it was time for lunch. My mother bundled up my little sister that day and they walked to school to meet me. They waited outside the lunchroom door, and when I saw my mother, I ran to her. Mom was wearing a yellow dress, covered with a black coat. Rebecca was clad in a cream-colored dress and brown jacket, and she held Mom's hand. We walked around the school grounds together as I ate lunch, and we talked.

"How are John and Sarah doing?" I asked.

"Why do you want to know about them?" asked Mom.

"You know," I said. "Because of what happened."

"They're doing okay," said my mother. "It's nice of you to ask. John looks so different now. He grew a beard."

"Do they talk to you about Jenny?"

"Sometimes Sarah does," said my mother. "But John doesn't talk much anymore."

Mom pulled a peanut butter sandwich with grape jam out of a little bag and handed it to me. As we walked, I munched on my sandwich.

"Sarah said their client Raymond West has tried to comfort them," said Mom. "He really liked Jenny."

After I finished my sandwich, Mom handed me a piece of white cake. She had made it a couple of days before for dessert. The cake was wrapped in wax paper and covered in white icing. I unwrapped it and took a bite. My mother smiled and wiped the icing from my cheeks. She handed me a small bottle of orange juice. I took a drink and wiped my mouth on my sleeve. She gave Rebecca something to drink, too.

"You'll probably see John and Sarah tomorrow," said Mom. "They'll come by our house with some papers for us to sign."

"Will it be after the Saturday morning cartoons?"

Mom smiled. "I think so."

We rounded the corner that led to the playground at the school. I hugged Mom. "I love you," I said.

"I love you too." She hugged me tight and patted me on the back. "I'll see you tonight."

The sights and sounds of children playing filled the schoolyard. I ran over to a group of classmates.

Before joining them, I glanced back at my mother. She smiled and waved to me. My little sister waved, too, and I waved back to them. Then Mom turned, picked up my little sister, and began the long walk back home. And gratitude filled my heart.

***

That Saturday morning, I awoke to hear my father coming home from the fire department. I ran downstairs to greet him. Dad was standing in the kitchen, dressed in a light-blue shirt with a red patch on the shoulder. His navy-blue pants and black boots completed his uniform. Dad's shiny badge caught the morning light. Mom had given him a cup of coffee with cream and sugar.

"Dad!"

"Hey, little rascal, how have you been?"

"Great!" I sniffed the air and smelled fresh-ground coffee and some kind of sweet pastry. "Did you bring donuts?"

"Yes, and I got your favorite—filled donuts."

My brothers came into the kitchen. Brad was wearing a green sweatshirt, and Ed had a striped button-up shirt. When Ed buttoned his shirt that morning, he had fastened each button off by one. And so, the collar on one side rose higher on top than the other. I started to say something about it, but I then noticed I had done the same thing.

"Dad brought donuts!" I shouted.

"Hurray!" they both said.

We opened the box and saw it was filled with delicious-looking donuts. There were glazed donuts along with coconut-covered cake donuts and chocolate-dipped donuts. They were brown, white, red, and rainbow-colored. Each one of us reached in to grab our favorite before it was gone. The donut I chose was filled with a cherry filling and dusted with powdered sugar. Dad asked me to bring him a glazed donut. I reached into the box to get one, but Ed grabbed it first.

"Dad asked me to get it!" I said.

"This is for me," said Ed.

"You already have a donut," said Brad.

"I want one for each hand," said Ed.

Reaching into the box, I searched for another glazed donut and brought it to my father. "How were your past three days?" I asked. "We missed you."

"It was okay," said Dad. "We had a fire Thursday night that was kind of scary."

"What happened?"

"Oh, it was a big building and I was inside searching for people. Flames were everywhere, and the smoke was thick. There were lots of rooms and I got twisted around."

"Oh no," said my mother. "I'm always afraid something like that will happen."

"How'd you get out?" I asked.

"Well, flames were all over the place, but I kept looking for an escape route. I searched and searched, but the smoke was so thick I couldn't see anything. As the flames closed in around me, I almost gave up. But just then I saw a flash of light. I went towards it and found a window. I broke it out and climbed to the ground outside." Dad shrugged. "No big deal."

"Harry," said my mother, her eyes wide. "Maybe it's time to retire. You can draw your pension when you're fifty-five years old. That's in two years. The houses are doing well. We could retire and move out of Kansas City."

"Where would we move to?" asked Brad.

"I've always wanted to retire to the country," said Dad. "Have a little farm. Raise horses, cattle, a few chickens. Have a big garden. That sort of stuff."

"That sounds great!" I said.

"Yeah, and maybe one day we will do it," said Dad.

"Could we have goats, too?" asked Ed.

"Maybe," said Dad.

"I'd like to get out of the city," said my mother. "There's so much crime. And firefighting is such dangerous work."

"Well, first we need to secure our income." Dad turned to my brothers and me. "That's why I appreciate your help fixing up the houses we buy."

"We'll keep helping," I said. "And maybe we can move to the country soon!"

"But for now, go play," said Mom. "John and Sarah will be here soon, and we have some business to discuss first."

Brad and Ed went outside. I went into the living room to watch Saturday morning cartoons. *The Bugs Bunny Show* was on and I sat in a red beanbag chair to watch it. Later would be *Land of the Lost, Star Trek: The Animated Series,* and my personal favorite, *Super Friends*. Halfway through the first cartoon, however, my brother Brad came into the living room.

"Jack, you want to play hide and seek with us?"

"Sure!"

"Great," he said. "The dogwood tree in the yard will be base."

We went out into the yard and over to the dogwood tree. Ed was already there waiting for us.

"Not it!" Ed yelled.

"Not it!" I shouted.

"Okay," said Brad. "You two hide first. You can hide anywhere, inside the house or outside."

Gravel popped in our driveway as John and Sarah pulled in. Sarah waved to us and walked to the front door of our home and knocked. John walked over to us.

"Hi," said Brad.

John nodded.

"Nice day," said Ed.

"So," John said. "Three brothers."

"Yeah," said Brad.

John looked us over. "Which one is the meanest?"

At the same time, Ed and I both said, "Brad."

Brad nodded his head in agreement.

"John," Sarah called over to him. "Mr. Kerrigan is ready for you."

John turned and followed Sarah into the front door of our house.

"Okay," said Brad. "Go!" He covered his eyes and started counting, "One, two, three ..."

Ed and I ran to the back door and went inside our home. We both charged into the storeroom where we kept canned goods.

"Get out!" said Ed. "I was here first!"

"No, you weren't!"

"Yes, I was!"

The backdoor opened.

"Shh!" I said. "Here he comes!"

Rushing out of the storeroom, I ran through the house and into the dining room, looking for a place to hide. The Prices and my parents were in the living room talking. I hurried into the guest room and hid under the bed. Listening hard, I waited for several minutes. Thinking it was time to sneak out and try to make it back to base, I started to slide out from under the bed. But just then, the door to the guest room opened. I stopped moving and listened. I didn't want Brad to catch me. But it wasn't Brad. My mother entered the guest room and she was talking with Sarah.

Mom and Sarah spoke softly and in serious tones. Although I couldn't make it at the time, my mother told me about Sarah's troubling request later. According to Mom, their conversation went something like this:

"I wanted to talk to you in private," said Sarah.

"What about?" said my mother.

"John and I have a little favor to ask you."

"Oh, yeah?"

"Yes."

There was a moment of silence.

"Go ahead."

"Look," said Sarah. "I'm just going to come right out and ask. Will you give us Rebecca?"

"What?" asked my mother. "What do you mean?"

"We want you to give us Rebecca."

"I'm afraid I don't understand."

"We want to have Rebecca," said Sarah. "To raise as our daughter. Give us Rebecca."

"Sarah, we can't do that."

"Why not? You have no problems having children. You can always have another one. But we have a hard time having babies. And I had a miscarriage. And Jenny died." Sarah paused. "So, anyway, we'd like to have Rebecca. Okay?"

"Sarah, I'm so sorry you've gone through such a hard time. I really am. And I'm sorry about Jenny. She was such a sweet little girl. But you can't have Rebecca."

There was a long silence.

"I'm sorry you feel that way," said Sarah.

"I hope you understand," said Mom.

A knock came at the guestroom door. The door opened and John's voice said, "Harry and I are all done with the paperwork."

"Okay," said Sarah.

"Did you finish your business with Betty?" John asked.

"John," said Sarah. "I've told you before. Don't call her Betty. And don't call him Harry. Call them Mr. and Mrs. Kerrigan."

They stepped out of the room, and I heard them talking as they walked towards the front door. When they we gone, I hurried out from under the bed. I ran through the house and out of the backdoor. Across the lawn was the dogwood tree and I ran towards it. Brad was coming around the back of the house, saw me, and charged after me. His feet thundered behind me and I ran as fast as I could. I tagged the tree, catching myself by pressing my hands against the trunk. Brad tagged my back, but I was safe.

"There's Ed!" he shouted and ran off to catch him.

John and Sarah were near their car and talking with my parents. My baby sister was playing near them. Sarah leaned down and said something to Rebecca. My stomach tightened. *My spider-sense was tingling.* I walked over to them and stopped about ten feet away.

"Rebecca," I called.

My little sister looked at me.

"Come on," I said, and put out my hand in her direction. "Come play hide and seek with us."

9
BACK TO THE LAND

The summer of 1977 brought change for my family. We had spent the past two years working towards our move to the country, which included stabilizing our finances. Dad's pension would provide our base income for the move, and our rental properties would augment that income. We had thirteen houses at the time, all of which were either being rented or were being sold through monthly payments.

We took several exploratory trips to the Ozark Mountains, which was four hours south of our home in Independence, Missouri. We then bought a large area of land with a house on it. The property was wild and untamed. Trees, deer, rabbits, and overgrown fields filled our land. I was very excited about our new adventure. The only problem left was how to manage all the houses we were renting in Kansas City.

And John Price was the answer.

My parents made a business arrangement with John and Sarah. They would manage our properties, collect the monthly payments, and send my family a check each month. In return, they would keep a percentage for their troubles. Since they had facilitated the buying of all of our houses, they were very familiar with the properties, tenants, and locations. It looked like a perfect solution. We could move to the country and carve out a life in the wilderness. We would be self-sufficient, or close to it. John and Sarah would stay in the city and earn some extra income for their efforts. It seemed like a win-win situation.

We made our move to the country during the heat of the summer. Outside of the yard surrounding our new home, the rest of the property was rough. I spent many happy days in the coming weeks exploring the forests, playing near the large pond, and camping in the fields.

A few weeks before the start of the fall semester, my parents took us to visit the local school. It was small, and the entire Elementary School consisted of a few classrooms branching off of a single hallway. My new teacher was there, and Mom took me to see her. After introductions, Mom asked about the reading program at the school.

"Jack reads well," Mom said. "He was in the advanced reading program at his last school. Could he do that here, too?"

"Advanced reading program?" asked my new teacher.

"Yes, he reads with the higher-grade students. He would like to continue that here, if possible."

My new teacher smiled and shook her head. "I'm glad he reads good, but we don't have nothing like that here."

School started the following week, but there was still a lot to do on our property. When the heat broke that summer, we began clearing our land. We kept as many trees as possible but made room for a barn, chicken house, and horse pen. Soon, we were raising chickens, ducks, and geese. We bought our first horse, a beautiful white mare named Dolly. We hired someone to mow our fields, and we built cattle and goat pens in the back and side pastures. Next, we bought an old tractor and plowed a large area of land into a garden. In season, we would plant all kinds of vegetables, such as corn, tomatoes, lettuce, watermelons, cucumbers, and squash. We also built rabbit cages and raised dozens of rabbits. Finally, on the southern side of our chicken house, we put in a home for doves. I fell in love with nature. It was such a wonderful change from the big city. Life was good.

The following year, we built a geodesic dome on our land. We also built a greenhouse and expanded our gardens. We plowed another tract of land and planted a wheat field. At harvest time, we cut the wheat by hand, flailed it, winnowed the chaff, ground the grain, and made homemade bread. We raised cattle and goats for fresh milk, too. Every morning before school, Ed and I would milk our herd. While we were at school, we let the cream rise to the top of the milk. Later, we scooped it off, churned the cream, and made our own butter from scratch. The hot, homemade bread, slathered in fresh butter, fed our bodies and souls at the same time.

I turned nine years old that year and became very interested in bees. I read several books on raising them and approached Dad about this possibility. My idea fit in well with my father's plans to be a country squire, and it didn't take much to convince him to order some bees. I waited patiently for them to arrive, and one day a box filled with buzzing bees came in the mail. Soon, my father and I were tending two hives, which would produce delicious dark honey for our family. We would drizzle the fresh nectar over our homemade bread and drink hot cups of fresh-brewed tea sweetened with honey.

One day, after working with our bees, my father and I sat on our porch. As we discussed the hive, the phone rang inside the house.

"I'll get it," said my mother's voice from inside.

After a few minutes, she came out to talk to my father.

"That was Sarah Price," said Mom.

"How are things going for them?" asked Dad.

"Not too bad. Remember their friend Raymond West?"

My father looked puzzled.

"He was the client of theirs who would wave at Jenny through the window of their office," said Mom. She paused, discerning if my father remembered him. "Raymond was the one who almost drowned in a flood a while back."

"Oh, okay."

"Anyway, John helped him move back into his home."

My father nodded. "How are our houses?"

"Pretty good," said my mother. "But they said a few tenants didn't pay us again this month, so our check will be a few hundred dollars short again."

"That's been happening every month for a while now."

"Yeah, but I told her it was okay. Those poor tenants are struggling to survive."

"Is it the same people every time?" I asked.

"No," said my mother. "Different tenants each time. It seems to cycle, though. Nearly every one of them has a turn. There's not quite a pattern, but almost."

"Well, everyone goes through hard times," said Dad. "I wouldn't expect John and Sarah to have to force them to pay."

"That's what I think," said Mom. She sat in a chair beside us. "Oh, and there's something else."

"What's that?" asked Dad.

"They want us to invest in a new business venture," said Mom.

"Another business idea."

Mom nodded.

"What do they want?" asked Dad.

"They want us to give them $50,000."

"What?" said Dad, surprised. "Why?"

"I'm not sure," said Mom. "They want to use the money to buy a private airplane."

"What for?" I asked.

"Something to do with Sarah's brother. They said a private plane would be a faster and cheaper way to do whatever business they have planned. It's weird, because she never mentioned having a brother before. Only a sister."

"Maybe he's just a friend who is like a brother," said Dad. "What did you tell them?"

"I told them we don't have that kind of money."

"And we wouldn't want to invest in something like that even if we did."

"I know," said Mom. There was a long pause. "By the way, they are coming here to visit."

"They're coming here?"

"Yes," said Mom.

"I hope they're not coming to pressure us to invest in an airplane for them."

"I don't think so. Sarah said she's only about an hour away from us, in Springfield. She said she was having a girls' night out with some friends." Mom paused. "But the odd thing is, John is with her."

"That is odd, for a girls' night out."

Mom nodded. "Her story is a little strange," said Mom. "And during our phone call, suddenly John's voice came on the line. He was listening in on an extension."

"Did you know he was listening in while you were talking?"

Mom shook her head. "I had no idea."

"I wish you would have told them 'No' about visiting," said my father.

"I know," said Mom. "But it caught me by surprise. It was an awkward situation."

Dad nodded his head. "Well," he said. "It's not a big deal. We'll have them over for a short visit, and then they'll be on their way."

"I hope so," said Mom.

A bee circled my father's head.

"Be careful," I said. "You don't want to get stung."

***

Our horse Dolly had stick-tights in her white mane. After carefully picking them out by hand, I ran a brush over her mane. Dolly stood still and let me brush all the stick-tights from her hair. As I brushed her, I patted her on her neck and back. When we were finished, I took a sugar cube from my pocket and stretched out my hand flat in front of her nose. Dolly sniffed the sugar cube and then nibbled it from my hand.

The gravel in our driveway crunched and popped under a car's tires. Our dogs started barking. Stepping out of our horse barn, I looked down our driveway. There was a car in our driveway, with a man and woman inside. It was John and Sarah Price. I patted Dolly and fed her a second sugar cube. Then I put her brush away and walked back towards our house.

Mom and Dad came out onto our porch to greet John and Sarah. As I walked up, Dad invited them to come inside.

"I'd like to see your property first," said John.

"Oh, okay," said Dad.

"I'm going inside with Mrs. Kerrigan," said Sarah.

Mom and Sarah went inside our home, and John smiled at me.

"Hi Jack," he said.

"Hi."

"I bet you know this land like the back of your hand."

Dad, John, and I walked towards a nearby forest.

"Wow," said John. "You have hundreds of trees."

"Yes," said Dad. "There were even more before we cleared some of them."

John pointed to a path leading into the thick forest. "I bet a man could hide out in there for a hundred years, and no one would ever find him."

Dad shrugged. "I guess so."

We walked around our property. We looked at our cattle, chickens, rabbits, and gardens.

"What's over there?" asked John. He pointed to a clump of trees to the west of our wheat field. "Another forest?"

"No," said Dad. "Jack and I planted an orchard there. Those are fruit trees. We planted apple, peach, and plum trees. And those are bush cherries next to the trees."

We walked through a clearing in a nearby forest that led past our goat pen. John didn't seem interested in the goats, and we walked back towards our house.

"How are our houses doing?" asked Dad.

"Not too bad," said John. "Sorry people don't pay every month."

"That's okay," said Dad. "I feel sorry for them."

We went inside the house. Mom had made a pot of coffee, and she was sitting with Sarah and drinking a cup. My little sister, Rebecca, sat next to my mother.

"Becky has grown so big," said Sarah.

"Yes," she said. "She's in kindergarten now."

"Too bad she can't live in Kansas City with us," said Sarah. There was an awkward pause. "The schools are better up there."

"We like it down here," said Mom.

"Don't you miss the big city?"

"No," said Mom. "We're happy here."

"John grew up not far from here," said Sarah.

"Oh, really?" said Dad. "Where?"

"On a small farm about an hour from here," said John.

"Like our place here?" asked Mom.

"No," said John. "We had no electricity, no running water, nothing like that."

"I told you about it before," said Sarah to my mother. "Remember?"

"Yes," said my mother. "I just didn't realize it was so close to here."

Sarah looked at Rebecca. "I brought you something."

"What is it?" said Rebecca.

"Come here," said Sarah.

Sarah clenched her hand, and she held it out in front of her. Rebecca walked over to her, and Sarah opened her hand. There was a beautiful jewel resting in her palm. Rebecca smiled and reached out for it.

"I would have given you one," Sarah said to my mother, "but that would be considered a bribe."

"And we would never do anything illegal," said John.

Sarah nodded. "But I can give it to Becky," she said.

Rebecca held the jewel up to the light, her eyes filled with wonder and delight.

"It's from India," Sarah said to Rebecca. "Do you like it?"

Rebecca smiled and nodded.

"What do you say?" said Mom to Rebecca.

"Thank you," said Rebecca.

"Sarah, where did you get such a beautiful ruby?" asked Mom.

"We're working on a side business," said Sarah. "Jewelry."

Many years later, my sister told us John and Sarah gave her several similar pieces of jewelry in private. They told her not to tell Mom and Dad. John and Sarah told her to trust them, that it would just be their "little secret." They said, "Don't tell Mommy." But back during this visit, we didn't know any of that was happening.

"You two have such creative business ideas," said my mother. "What are you two doing after this?"

"We have some business to do near Joplin," said John. "Then we are heading back to Kansas City." John looked at Sarah. "In fact, we need to be going."

"That's right," said Sarah, and she stood up. "Thank you for letting us see your hideout here in the country."

My parents walked John and Sarah to the door, and Rebecca and I followed behind.

"So, back to Kansas City," said Dad as they were leaving.

"Yes," said John, digging the car keys out of his pocket.

"And after that," said Sarah, "we're going to India."

"India?" said Dad.

"Yes," said John.

"When are you leaving for India?" asked Mom.

"Soon," said John.

"Our plan is for me to fly out first, and John will come a week later."

"Why don't you both go at the same time?" asked Mom.

"It will be better this way," said John. He shrugged. "It's complicated."

They walked over to their car and got inside.

"I don't understand," said my mother. "Why not go together?"

John started the car. Sarah looked back at my mother and smiled.

"John has something he needs to tie up first."

10
THE MURDER OF RAYMOND WEST

1978

The scorching August sun flickered through the branches of a tall oak as I rode my horse through a grove of trees. Because of the heat, she and I stayed near the forest. We kept our rides short during the summer to keep Dolly cool. After riding for twenty minutes in the early morning, I took Dolly back to the barn. She had a long drink of water and nibbled some hay. After I removed her saddle, I brushed her down and patted her. Reaching into my pocket, I pulled out a sugar cube and gave it to her. When Dolly was cared for and comfortable, I went back to our house. In the living room, Mom and Dad were talking. When I entered the room, they stopped speaking.

"What's wrong?" I asked.

Mom looked at Dad, and he shrugged his shoulders.

"John's been arrested," said Mom.

"What for?"

"They've arrested him for murder," said Dad.

"Murder?" My stomach tightened. "Who did he murder?"

"Maybe no one," said Dad.

"Do you remember Raymond West?" said Mom. "He was the retired truck driver who used to wave at Jenny through the window of their office. He lived nearby them."

"I remember hearing about him."

"Well, he's been murdered."

"And they think John did it?"

"Yes," said Dad. "But a person is innocent until proven guilty."

John and Sarah were more than just business associates with my parents. I knew they thought of them as friends, and so I felt bad for Mom and Dad. But at the same time, I always worried about my parents when they were alone with him. John made me feel uncomfortable, and I never trusted him. I had a lot of feelings on hearing the news that they had arrested him for murder, but surprise was not one of them.

"Sarah called and wanted us to give her money to bail John out of jail," said Mom.

"But we can't do that," said my father.

Mom nodded. "And Sarah wanted us to be a character witness for John at the trial," she said. "But we don't feel we can do that either."

"I wonder what happened," I said.

"The details are sketchy," said Dad.

"The last time West was seen, he talked to a neighbor," said Mom. "West told the neighbor he was feeling sick."

"Maybe it was natural causes," Dad said. "You never know."

"Well," said Mom. "Except when they found his body, he had been tortured and dismembered."

"That seems weird if it was natural causes," I said.

"I know," said Mom. "But there were no stabs marks or bullet wounds." She shook her head. "He had been missing for too long. When they finally found him, they couldn't determine a cause of death."

Dad nodded. "We may never know what really happened, but I'd like to find out."

***

It wasn't until decades later, when I was an adult, that I learned the details of the murder of Raymond West. My father studied the case. Over coffee one beautiful spring day, he told me what he had discovered.

According to Dad's research, a man named Charles Banker became concerned about West's absence. Banker was a close friend of Raymond West, and something didn't seem right. So, he went to West's home and knocked on the door, but there was no response. West's car was there, however, adding to the mystery. Charles Banker looked around for anything unusual. Noticing a window shade was raised, he looked through it. He saw an unmade bed, but nothing else caught his eye. Mr. Banker became concerned about his friend. He had known him for over thirty years. So, he called the police and filed a missing person's report. The police began looking into the matter. Their initial investigation revealed someone who would become a person of interest.

"That person was John Price," my father said, pouring a cup of steaming hot coffee.

"I remember when that happened," I said, taking a sip from my cup.

My father nodded. "When the police interviewed John, he told them Raymond West was simply out-of-town with his girlfriend. He said the couple were spending a few days in the Ozarks and would be back soon."

I bobbed my head. "That probably seemed like a rational explanation to the officers, and believable."

"But when Charles Banker returned to his friend's house," said Dad, "he discovered a few significant changes since he was last there."

"What did he find?" I asked. I drank the last of my coffee and got up to pour a fresh cup.

"Well, he noticed there was a note on the door that wasn't there before," said Dad. "It was written on the letterhead from John and Sarah's tax business. The note said Raymond West would be out of town for a few days, and to contact John if needed."

"Very interesting."

My father nodded, then continued. "Mr. Banker then checked the house and noticed a second change from the last time he had been there. The bedroom window shade that was previously raised had been pulled down."

As I stirred a little cream and sugar into my cup, my father told me more. He said something about all this just didn't feel right to Charles Banker. Not only had someone been there since his last visit, but John's story didn't make sense. In all the years Banker had known him, Ray West had never had a girlfriend, and it was unlikely he ever would. West also never left town without telling Charles. Since Mr. Banker had filed a missing person's report, he felt he needed to be proactive and follow up with the police. He contacted them again, and the police agreed to enter West's home to investigate further. Banker's persistence and cooperation with the police would prove to be key to locating his missing friend.

"When the police entered West's home," said Dad, "they found what seemed to be a normal house. In the living room, however, there was something of interest. On the coffee table, there was a handwritten note."

"What did it say?" I took a sip of my coffee.

"It said Ray was sleeping late, and not to disturb him. That would explain a lot, especially considering a neighbor reported Ray was feeling sick."

We were quiet for a moment. Dad added another sugar cube to his cup, and handed one to me. Stirring it in, I inhaled the rich scent of the dark Columbian roast. As we drank our coffee, Dad continued telling me about his findings.

He said Charles Banker was with the police when they found the note. Mr. Banker noticed two odd features about it. For starters, it was not written in West's handwriting. If that wasn't enough, it also was signed "Raymond." But Banker knew his friend almost always signed his name "Ray." The only exception was when he signed checks.

"But when he signed checks," said Dad, "he used his full, legal first name."

"Raymond," I said, thinking about the implications.

Dad nodded. "All this was suspicious," he said, "but there was nothing else the police could do at that point."

"I guess not."

"But Charles Banker had an idea. He installed padlocks on West's door and gave one set of keys to the police. But as he and a helper were installing the locks on the door, John Price came up and confronted them."

"What did he say?"

"John demanded to know what Charles Banker was doing," said Dad. "Tempers flared, but fortunately, the heated situation quickly cooled."

Dad refilled his cup. As he did so, he continued telling me details about the case. Dad said that after a brief discussion, John drove off in his car, and the encounter seemed over. But it wasn't. According to Banker and his helper, John didn't actually leave. Instead, he secretly moved his car behind a nearby delivery truck. When the driver of the delivery truck had finished his business, he drove away, revealing John Price. John sat there in his car for several more minutes, and then he drove away.

"Things were quiet for the next two weeks," Dad said. "But on August 14th, Banker returned to his friend's home. He examined the house, and he discovered something troubling. There was dried blood in a bedroom, and the house smelled terrible. Banker contacted the police again, and they came to investigate further."

"Oh, wow," I said.

"This time, the police search of West's home found disturbing evidence of foul play. In the basement, they discovered a garbage bag. In the bag, they found bloody sheets, eyeglasses, and other personal items. There was also a lawn chair, stained with human blood."

"That's horrible." I set my cup down. I wasn't in the mood for coffee.

"And there's more," said Dad. "Upstairs, the police found a suspicious stain that made them decide to check out the attic. It was there they came upon a grisly scene. The decomposing body of Raymond West."

Dad sat his cup down, too. It was half full, but I could tell he was finished with it. He waited a moment and then continued.

"Raymond West had been dismembered. His torso had been partly wrapped in a plastic bag and tied with a rope. His head was draped in sheets, wrapped with a cord, and his limbs lay nearby. They also found pulleys and rope in the attic, along with other items that may have been used to torture West."

"What did the police do?"

"Well, a few hours after finding the body, the police handcuffed John and brought him to the police station. They found something that made him the prime suspect."

"That's interesting." I leaned forward in my seat. "Go on."

"John was the payee of a $5000 check, signed by Raymond West," said Dad. "What's more, the check was dated Sunday, July 23, 1978."

"That was the same day West went missing."

"That's right," said Dad. "During police questioning, John would claim that the check from West was a loan for him to expand his tax business. After hours of interrogation, John was released, but remained the prime suspect. The police had his fingerprints and a sample of his handwriting, but that was all."

"So, they let him go."

"That's my understanding," said Dad. "But the very next day after his release, the police questioned John again. He agreed to let the police conduct a search, which revealed some interesting clues."

"Fascinating. What did they find?"

"In his car, they found several of West's checks, a trash bag, papers with West's name, and twenty feet of rope. John was once again brought in to the police station for questioning, but he denied murdering Raymond West."

"Of course."

"Right, of course. But his denial wasn't enough to keep the authorities from charging John with murder. During this time, Sarah Price contacted us and asked us for bail money and to be character witnesses for John at his trial. But we declined both requests."

"I remember that."

"You probably remember better than I do," Dad smiled. "So, they set John's trial date for October. But during the pretrial stage of the legal process, John's attorney pointed out to the court something important."

"They didn't read him his Miranda Rights."

"That's right. And since the police hadn't read John his Miranda Rights, all the evidence they gathered after his arrest was inadmissible in court." Dad shrugged. "Regardless of how persuasive it may have been. This and other irregularities led to the charges being dropped and the case being dismissed."

"It's surprising they would have made such a simple mistake."

"Yes, but it was a tough case," said Dad. "Prosecutor James Bell made a statement to reporters after the case was dismissed. He described the entire situation as one of the most complex and mysterious cases he had ever worked on."

"So," I said. "The trial was over before it had begun."

My father poured out the cold liquid from his cup and refilled it with fresh, hot coffee. He picked up a clean mug, poured in fresh coffee, and handed it to me. I held the cup, its heat warming my hands, but I didn't feel like drinking it.

"That's right," said Dad. "After all that, they were back to square one. John Price was a free man."

***

Back in 1978, Brad, Ed, and I raked the autumn leaves into a huge pile. We took turns jumping into the mountain of red, yellow, and orange. Every so often, we would stop and rake up the leaves again. When the sun began to set, I built a campfire near my tent site. I roasted marshmallows over the fire and shared them with my little sister. I was ten years old that fall, and proud to be trusted with the campfire. Mom and Dad came out to check on us and sat with us by the fire.

"Are you two having fun?" asked Mom.

"Uh-huh," said Becky. "Jack is making me marshmallows."

"Yum," said Mom. "I love marshmallows cooked over a campfire."

"Me too," said Becky.

"What are you two talking about?" she asked.

"Not much," said Becky.

There was a long silence.

"Any news on the murder trial?" I asked.

"Yes, Sarah called your mother about it."

"What's happening with it?"

"She said they dropped the charges against John," said Mom.

"Hmm," I said, handing her a roasted marshmallow. "Did she say why?"

"Yeah." Mom took a bite of the marshmallow. "Ouch! That's hot."

"Not too hot for me," said Becky.

"Here you go." Mom handed my little sister the marshmallow I had given her.

"Thanks!" said Becky, and began eating the toasted marshmallow.

"Why did they let John go?" I asked.

"Sarah said they didn't have a shred of evidence against him," said Mom.

"That's weird," I said. "I wonder why they arrested him then."

"That happens sometimes in cases like this," said Dad. "There is a lot of pressure on the police to find the killer fast."

"So, what is John going to do now?"

Dad shrugged his shoulders. "Apparently he's going to start another business," he said. "John knows a guy from India and they are starting it together."

"Doing what?"

"I'm not sure," said Dad. "Something to do with the pharmaceutical industry." He paused and looked at me. "Do you know what that is? Companies that make and sell medicines."

"Oh, okay," I said.

"Yeah," said Dad. "Their business has something to do with medicine tablet machines. Installing some kind of tablet-making thing." He shrugged. "I guess to make medicine pills or something like that. I don't know exactly."

"Yuck," said Becky. "I don't like medicine."

Mom smiled. "Me neither."

"So, the trial's over?" I asked, as the orange light from the flickering campfire slowly began to fade.

"I think so," said Dad. He took a deep breath and let it out. "I hope the killings are over."

Nodding my head, I stirred the dying embers of the campfire with a stick. I glanced up at Dad and saw his brow was furrowed. He was staring at the coals. I tossed the stick into the fire. "I hope they are over, too."

But the murders were just beginning.

11
AVENGING ANGELS

The morning light shone through our classroom window. It reflected off the white walls, which had been repainted that fall. The room was hot, even though it was November. Mrs. Brown, our Fourth-Grade teacher, stood before us. She was wearing a light-blue dress and looking through her notes. Her blond hair was showing grey at the temples, and scooped back in a ponytail. She cleared her throat and ran her fingers through her hair. After a moment, she called the class to order and we became quiet.

"I'm sure some of you have been following the news."

"You mean about what happened in South America?" asked Keri.

"That's right," said Mrs. Brown. "In Guyana."

"What happened?" asked Bobby.

"There was a cult leader there who made his followers commit mass suicide," said Keri.

"Yes," said Mrs. Brown. "First, they shot Congressman Leo Ryan and others. Then their leader ordered them to commit suicide. They were told to drink grape punch laced with cyanide."

"What's cyanide?" asked Bobby.

"It's a chemical that stops your body from absorbing oxygen," I said.

Mrs. Brown nodded. "Several hundred there committed forced suicide."

"If they forced them to do it," I said, "why are they calling it suicide?"

"What do you mean?"

"If they were made to do it, wasn't it murder?"

"That's a good question," said Mrs. Brown. "But whether it was mass murder or mass suicide, it was still a tragedy."

The classroom was quiet. My stomach was upset. I glanced around at the other students. Most of them were looking down. Some were gazing out the classroom window. At least one child was crying.

After a few moments, our teacher continued. Mrs. Brown had followed the news closely. She told us the leader's name was Jim Jones. He was a radical American minister who formed a cult called the Peoples Temple. His followers were fanatic in their devotion to Jones and followed him to the jungles of South America. Jones wanted to form a community far from civilization. They called it Jonestown after its founder.

"There were a lot of red flags," she told us. "For instance, Jim Jones would occasionally require loyalty tests."

"What's a loyalty test?" asked Bobby.

"He would make them rehearse mass suicide."

"I don't understand," said Keri.

"They would drink a flavored punch that they were told was poisoned with cyanide," said Mrs. Brown. "But it wasn't really. Well, at least not until the final time."

"How did Jim Jones get the cyanide?" I asked.

"Jones had a jeweler's license; that allowed him to buy cyanide to clean gold. They tested it on pigs to find the proper dose."

This sparked me to thinking. My parents had told me John and Sarah Price had a side business in jewelry. They had given a beautiful ruby to my little sister when they visited us. Also, they had a book with an article on using cyanide as a poison. I wondered if John ever worked with it. My mind also thought of Raymond West's murder. The medical examiners didn't find bullet or knife wounds. *Could he have been poisoned?*

Mrs. Brown continued speaking, drawing me out of my thoughts. She told us about how what began as a small church group evolved into something deadly.

"Over time," she said, "concerns about abuse and members being held against their will emerged in the outside world. To investigate, Congressman

Ryan led a delegation to visit Jonestown. At first, the visit seemed to go well. Ryan was preparing to leave, and some members of the group asked him to help them escape Jonestown."

"Where did they want to go?" asked Keri. "To Russia?"

"No, they wanted to return to the United States."

"Wow," said Keri.

"Anyway, the shootings began while they were trying to leave by airplane," Mrs. Brown said. "Jim Jones ordered the people he called his 'Avenging Angels' to murder them at the airfield. Ryan and others were shot and killed. It was horrible."

My stomach tightened; my shoulder muscles were tensed and my jaw was firm. I tried to relax my muscles, but they still felt taut. I took a deep breath and let it out. I raised my hand.

"Yes, Jack?"

"Is that when Jones forced the cult members to commit suicide?" I asked.

"That's right," said Mrs. Brown. "Back in the compound, they gave the remaining members grape punch to drink, laced with cyanide. Most of them drank it. Mothers were told to give it to their babies first and then drink it themselves. And they did."

"Oh, no," said Bobby.

Mrs. Brown nodded. "Over nine hundred were dead in a matter of minutes. Only seven survived."

"How about the children?" asked Keri.

Mrs. Brown was quiet for a moment. She swallowed hard. "Three-hundred children were killed."

"Why would someone do something like that?" I asked her. "How could they?"

"I don't know," she replied. "I think his 'Avenging Angels' were brainwashed. They probably believed they were doing a good deed and fighting evil."

"By shooting those innocent people?"

"I'm afraid so."

I shook my head. "But what about Jim Jones?"

"I think it must go back to his childhood," said Mrs. Brown. "They say he grew up in extreme poverty. As a child, he lived in a shack without plumbing."

John Price grew up in a shack without electricity or plumbing, too, I thought. "But it must be more than that," I said aloud. "A lot of people grow up in poverty, and they turn out fine. Some of them even become extraordinary. Like Abraham Lincoln."

"You're right," said Mrs. Brown. "I'm sure we'll learn more about Jim Jones over time. Maybe it had nothing to do with his environment. Maybe some people are just born that way."

"Born what way?" I asked.

Mrs. Brown shrugged her shoulders. "Made for murder."

"I hope that isn't true," I said.

Keri raised her hand.

"Yes, Keri?"

"Why would people join a cult?" asked Keri.

"Well," said Mrs. Brown, "the group began with good intentions. In the early days, they wanted racial equality and social justice. Those are both good things. But over time, they became more extreme, and it became more and more about Jim Jones. They became his Avenging Angels. They drank the Flavor Aid in more ways than one."

"I wouldn't have drunk it," said Bobby, shaking his head. "No way."

"What would you have done?" asked Keri.

Bobby looked serious. "I would have said 'no'."

"Me too," said several others.

"You think that now," said Mrs. Brown. "But the truth is, you really don't know what you would do in that situation. It all began in a relatively normal church setting. They were outside the mainstream, but that's all. But things slowly changed. Bit by bit, the message became more radical. To fit in with the group, people needed to adapt. By the time it was too late, it all made perfect sense to them. And they drank the Flavor Aid."

"But that's the scary part," I said. "You know what I mean? It's scary that normal people could become so irrational. That the group could sway them so much. They went so far it even seemed like a good idea for them to commit suicide."

"Or murder," said Keri. "Like with Charles Manson."

"That's right," said Mrs. Brown. "I hope that's a lesson you all take from this. Some people—"

Mrs. Brown stopped and turned her head. Suddenly, emotion was heavy in the air and we all sat in silence. Although she was looking away from us, I could tell she was crying. After a moment, she wiped her cheek and turned back to face us. Her eyes were red as she gazed at us.

"Remember this," she said to the class. "If someone asks you for blind faith, you'd be a fool not to take a peek."

A knock came at our classroom door. It was Bobby's mother.

"Oh, that's right," said Mrs. Brown. She smoothed her blue dress and brushed her blond hair back with her fingers. "Today is Bobby's birthday, and his mother brought cake and drinks."

"Hurray!" we all shouted.

As Bobby's mother passed around the cake and drinks, we all sang happy birthday to Bobby. We began eating our cake, talking, and laughing. After a few moments, Bobby looked at me.

"Well, this is awkward," he said, holding up his drink. He smiled sheepishly.

I looked down into my cup and glanced back at Bobby. I said what we were both thinking.

"It's grape Flavor Aid."

***

The school was only three miles from our house, but it took an hour and a half to ride home on the school bus. The bus drove over miles of dirt roads, dropping off students along the way. Our house was the last stop, and we were the only students on the school bus by the time we reached home. Bouncing along the dusty roads, I thought of Jim Jones and his Avenging Angels. I wondered: *How could a killer delude himself into thinking he was doing something good? Is that how the forces of darkness operate? Through small changes over time?* The smell of burning grass filled the air. As we crested over the last hill, we passed through a cloud of thick smoke. Fear seized me as the smoke cleared, revealing our burning fields.

"Oh, no!" I shouted. "Look!"

Most of our western field was black, burned down to the roots. Near our house, my mother and father were fighting the flames as they moved closer and closer to our home. Our bus came to a stop, and we hurried off. We ran up the driveway and to the fire line.

"Get back!" shouted my mother. "Keep Rebecca away!"

"Did you call the fire department?" called Brad, his eyes wide with terror.

"Yes," yelled my mother. "But it's just a little volunteer fire department. They're coming, but they have to get the volunteers first."

My brothers and I grabbed shovels and rakes and began fighting the fire. The flames danced all around us as we worked. My mother turned on the water hose and sprayed the ground on the side of our house facing the fire.

"Oh, no!" my sister yelled. "The cows!"

On the edge of our western field was a cattle corral. We had ten Holstein calves living there, and the fire was running along one side of their pen. They pressed against the other side, staying as far as possible from the flames. My heart pounded within me. Dropping my shovel, I ran to the pen and struggled to unlatch the gate. It was jammed, so I kept hitting it with the palm of my hand. The calves mooed, their desperate cries filling the smoky air. As the fire entered the paddock, the cattle panicked and charged towards the gate. I struck the latch with all my might, and it gave way. The gate swung open, and the calves ran through it to safety.

Just then, the local volunteer fire department pulled up. Dad waved to them to drive through our yard to the fire line. The firetruck was small and very old, nothing like the ones I used to climb on in Kansas City. The men leaped out of the old firetruck, uncoiled the water hose, and pointed it at the fire. They braced for the surge of high-pressure water, but nothing happened.

"Turn it on!" shouted a firefighter.

"I did!" shouted another.

One man climbed onto the truck and looked at the water pressure gage.

"Oh no," he said. He looked at us. "There's no pressure."

"I'm sorry," said another man. "Without water pressure, there's nothing we can do."

My father pointed at a firefighter. "You," he said. "Get a shovel and start on the far right and work your way down the line."

"Right," said the man. He grabbed a shovel from the firetruck and ran to the right side of the flames.

"The rest of you, start next to him and work your way down the line."

"I'm the captain," said one of the men. "I give the orders here."

"He's a Kansas City fire captain," said my mother. "Do what he tells you."

The men looked to their captain for an order, but he stood staring at the flames.

My father turned and addressed the firemen directly. "Get shovels. Now!"

The men ignored their captain and did as my father commanded. They grabbed shovels and other tools and lined up near their fellow firefighter. Dad ran up and down the line, giving them instructions on how to fight the fire. Working together, they soon had the flames under control.

A few hours later, Dad and I walked over the blackened fields. As we walked, we saw several snakes had survived the fire, but now had no place to hide.

"I'm so glad we stopped the fire before it reached our home," said Dad, stepping over a garter snake.

"Me too," I said. I looked around at the field, black as coal from the fire. "After all those years of fighting fires in Kansas City, it would have been terrible to have our home burn down here."

Dad nodded. "Well," he said, laying his hand on my shoulder. "That was enough excitement for one day. I hope the world holds together from now on." He looked at me and smiled.

But what we didn't know as we stood in the charred field that day was that soon the entire world would change forever. The fire was over, but the flames were just beginning.

PART II
THE 1980s
DURING THE CHANGE

12
SEVEN MORE MURDERS

September, 1982

Dan threw a left hook at my jaw, and then he ducked to the right.

Blocking his left hook with my right hand, I jabbed back at him twice with my left. He blocked my left jabs and then threw a right cross at my face. Not wanting his powerful fist to connect, I blocked his swing with my left hand and stepped to the side.

Dan pivoted to my left and threw a powerful right hook at my jaw. I raised my left fist to block it, but it caught me on my chin. As it connected, I rolled hard to my left, reducing the impact of the blow.

Punching back at his jaw twice more with my left jab, I saw him raise his right hand slightly to protect his face, leaving his stomach open. I was only fourteen years old, and Dan was seventeen. He was five inches taller than me and had twenty pounds of weight in his favor; I knew his jaw wasn't my best target. Turning my hip to put all my weight behind it, I threw a right jab at his stomach. It connected, and Dan stumbled back, winded.

Coach Johnson blew his whistle. "That's it! Good job, guys."

Eye of the Tiger by the band Survivor was blaring over the stereo as we sparred. Our coach called to the boy sitting near the boombox. "Kill it!"

There was no response, so Coach Johnson blew his whistle and yelled again. "Jackson! Jackson! Kill the music!"

Bob Jackson glanced at our coach, gave him a thumbs-up, and turned off the music.

Coach Johnson mumbled to himself, "This is kid's boxing club, not *Rocky IV the Musical*." He shook his head. "Geez."

Dan and I took off our boxing gloves and shook hands.

"Jack, good job. Keep up the footwork when you are boxing a taller opponent. He's got the height and weight advantage on you, but you're faster."

"Okay, coach," I said, and nodded. "Thanks."

"Dan," said our coach. "Good work. You've got a powerful right cross. But don't forget to keep your guard up."

Coach Johnson raised his fists to demonstrate. "Block your stomach with your elbows and keep your gloves up to protect your face. Like this."

Dan nodded. "I know, but I was hoping for an uppercut."

"Don't try so hard for his jaw," said our coach. "Notice what Jack did. Takedown the body, and the head will go with it."

Dan nodded. "Thanks, coach."

"Keep up the good work, men." Coach Johnson blew his whistle. "Next! Jackson, hit the music!"

Two other guys took our place and began sparring. *Eye of the Tiger* boomed from the stereo. Dan and I walked towards the locker room to shower and get changed for our next class.

"Man, I've got a terrible headache," said Dan. "Do you have a painkiller?"

I shook my head. "You could ask at the nurse's office."

Dan nodded and rubbed his temples. We stopped at the water fountain, and we took turns taking a long drink. I drank first and then waited for Dan. When he had finished, he wiped his mouth and looked at me.

"Hey, did you see the news?" he asked.

"I'm not sure," I said. "What about?"

"The murders."

"No, what happened?"

"Someone is killing people in Chicago."

My muscles tightened. "Oh no, do you know any details?"

Dan shrugged. "Not really. People are dying and they don't know why. That's all I know right now. Watch the news tonight."

"I will."

We continued walking toward the locker room. Our conversation quickly turned to more mundane matters. We spoke about an upcoming history assignment, a teacher we didn't care for, and a Stephen King novel Dan was reading. I told Dan about the old motorcycle my parents had given me, and the big box of classic comics they bought for a dollar at a garage sale.

"Man, that's awesome," said Dan. "If you want me to check the price guide on any of them, let me know."

"Absolutely," I said, and smiled.

Dan collected comics and knew a great deal about their value and history. That was where my interest was at that age, too. We loved reading about the adventures of superheroes as they fought against evil; their adventures inspired us. But unbeknownst to us, more serious matters were stirring. The world was about to change forever.

Dan's words about the murders in Chicago that day were the first hints of a mystery that began that autumn and continues on to this day.

***

When I got home, I was torn between two of my favorite wind-down activities. One was the huge cardboard box filled with hundreds of old comic books. Vintage Batman, Superman, and many others were in excellent condition. That autumn, I spent many wonderful afternoons sitting out by our pond or under a shady tree, reading fantastic tales of high adventure. The other option was my beat-up Yamaha dirt bike. My parents bought it for almost nothing, and I learned to ride on that old motorcycle. I loved the feeling of the wind in my face, and I would spend many happy hours riding over our fields and on the dirt roads near our home.

The weather was nice that late autumn day, so my dirt bike won out. I kick-started the motorcycle, and its two-stroke engine roared to life. The smell of gasoline and the purr of the motor made me smile. For the next hour, I rode over our hills and on nearby dirt roads. I had been practicing doing wheelies and was getting pretty good at it. I also loved to aim my motorcycle at a steep dirt pile, fly a few feet off the ground when I hit it, and land in the pasture beyond. When I returned home, my parents were sitting on the porch, drinking iced tea.

"How was school today, Jack?" asked my mother.

"It was fine," I said.

"Pour yourself a glass of tea."

There were clean glasses on the little white table. Next to them was a pitcher of sweet tea with ice cubes and sliced lemons floating on top. I poured a glass of tea and sat by my parents.

"Dan said there was something interesting on the news," I said. I took a sip of sweet tea.

"Do you mean the murders in Chicago?" asked my mother.

"Yeah. Do you know anything about it?"

"Oh yes, it's scary," she said. "We've been following it closely."

"It all began a few days ago, on the 29th," said Dad. "A young girl awoke one morning with a sore throat."

"Her name was Mary Kellerman," said Mom. "She was only 12 years old." Mom shook her head. "She was feeling sick, so she did what many of us would do in the same situation. She went to her family's medicine cabinet and looked for a painkiller."

"What happened?"

Dad got up and refilled his glass. As he poured, he continued. "Well, she found a bottle of Extra-Strength Tylenol, popped the top off, and opened the medicine bottle," he said. "She measured out two capsules into her hand and took them with some water."

"Something we've all done a hundred times," I said.

"Right," said Dad. He sat down next to Mom. "But little did she know that a crazy person had laced the medicine with cyanide poison."

My stomach felt like I had just taken a left jab to my solar plexus. "Oh no."

Mom nodded. "Within moments, she collapsed. Paramedics worked hard to revive her, but couldn't."

"That's so sad," I said. The girl's parents came to my mind, and how they must have felt losing their daughter so young.

"Mary Kellerman was the first to die that day," said Dad. "But she wasn't the last. A 27-year-old postal worker—"

"Adam Janus," said Mom.

"That's right," said Dad. "Adam Janus, poor guy. Anyway, he was next to die in this tragedy. That morning, he had a chest cold. He took Tylenol laced with cyanide, and died later that same day."

"But it didn't end there," said Mom. "The story gets worse."

"What happened next?"

"That evening, Adam's family met in his home," said Dad. "Shocked at Adam's tragic death, his brother—"

"Stanley," said my mother.

"Right," said Dad. "Stanley had a headache. And so did Theresa, Adam's sister-in-law."

"Probably caused by the stress of the sudden death," I said.

Mom looked serious. "So, they checked the medicine cabinet and found a bottle of Tylenol. Soon, they were both dead as well."

"Wow," I said. My stomach tightened; tingles crept up my spine.

"But the tragedy wasn't over yet," said Dad. "A woman named Mary Reiner had recently given birth."

"She was the same age as Adam Janus," said Mom. She looked sad. "All the victims were so young."

"Mary had body aches, and took Tylenol she had bought at a store in Winfield," said Dad. "These capsules were also laced with cyanide. Soon she was dead, leaving four children behind."

"I hope that's all," I said. Silently, I prayed for the victims.

"It's not," said Mom. "A woman named Mary McFarland also died after taking the tainted medicine. She was just thirty-one. She collapsed in her office in front of her co-workers. Like with the others, nothing could be done to save her."

"And later that night," said Dad, "a young flight attendant returned home to Chicago after a hard night's work. Little did she know she would be the next victim that day of an unknown killer." He turned to Mom. "What was her name?"

"Paula Prince," said Mom. "She went to a Walgreens store near her home. That night she too took the tainted Tylenol. She was the seventh victim."

"Seven murdered in one day," I said. I couldn't believe someone could be so cruel. "How did they discover the Tylenol was poisoned?"

"Well, that's a good question," said Dad. "While all this was happening, two firefighters noticed something. There were similarities between the deaths of the three members of the Janus family. One of them also noticed that all three had taken Tylenol."

"And there was a nurse," said Mom.

"That's right," said Dad. "Helen Jensen."

"Right," said Mom. She paused and finished her glass of tea. "She investigated the Janus murders and first suggested the Tylenol in Adam's home had been poisoned."

"Wow," I said. "That's brilliant."

"It was a lucky guess," said Mom.

"Or an educated one," I responded. I thought for a moment. "So, the killings were random?"

"Apparently," said Mom.

"Which is strange," said Dad. "Hard to figure out a motive for a random murder."

"Maybe it wasn't random," I said. "Maybe it just looks that way."

"What do you mean?"

I shrugged my shoulders. "I don't know. It could be anything. Maybe one person was the intended victim, and the others were killed to make it seem random."

"To throw them off the case," said Mom.

"Yeah," I said. "Or maybe it was some other motive we haven't thought of yet."

"Like what?" asked Dad.

"I don't know." I shrugged. "Maybe they hated the company that makes Tylenol. Maybe they have a grudge against them."

"It's almost time for the nightly news. Do you want to watch with us tonight, Jack?" asked Mom.

"Sure."

We went inside and spent several minutes chopping squash, mushrooms, onions, and other vegetables. Mom boiled rice and sautéed the fresh veggies in a skillet with a little olive oil. The warm scent of the spices and cooking vegetables filled the air and made my mouth water. It was done in a few minutes, and we brewed a pot of hot tea to go with it. We ate together at the dining room table, laughing and talking about our day. When the meal was over, we went into the living room to watch television. The newscast opened with news about the Tylenol murders.

"Terror seizes the nation as police search frantically for the unknown killer of seven people in the Chicago area."

"Here we go," said Mom, glancing at me. "I hope they catch him soon."

"Me too."

"Meanwhile, Americans panic as they empty their medicine chests out of fear of over-the-counter products tainted with deadly cyanide."

"Do we have any Tylenol right now?" I asked.

"No," said Mom. "I got rid of it."

"Good."

The news continued, recapping the recent murders. It reported the mass recall of Tylenol products, and it described similar copycat crimes around the nation.

"Other cases involving product tampering have been reported in several states, including California, Florida, Ohio, and Colorado."

"Oh no," I said.

"Mouthwash, eyedrops, and other similar products have been tainted with acid."

"I was afraid that would happen," said Dad. "There are always copycat killers."

"One question haunts both police and citizens alike."

The tension was high in the room as the news anchor looked into the camera and spoke directly to a terrified nation.

"Who is the cyanide killer?"

13
THE FACELESS FURY

The next day, the school bell rang, and we all went to our seats.

Amy Smith wore overalls over a white t-shirt and had short red hair. She held a cup of soda in her hand and was trying to finish it before class began. She took a big gulp, lowered the cup, and looked inside.

"Tastes weird," Amy said. She smelled it, wrinkled her nose, and took another sip.

A small group of classmates giggled.

"What's so funny?" asked Amy.

"Randall put something in it," said Shannon, a thin blond girl with a ponytail hanging in the back.

"What did you put in it, Randell?" asked Amy.

"Cyanide!" said Randell, and the class erupted in laughter.

We all fell silent as our teacher entered the classroom.

"Mrs. Sanders, Randell put something in Amy's cup," said Shannon. "I saw him."

"What did you put in her cup, Randell?" asked our teacher. Mrs. Sanders was in her mid-thirties and had curly brunette hair. She was wearing a lime-green pantsuit. She pushed up her sleeves as she stood there looking at Randell. "Well, I'm waiting."

Randell squirmed in his chair and tapped his dirty black cowboy boots against the floor. His wrinkled Iron Maidan t-shirt had a picture of a demon named *Eddie* on the front. The words, *The Number of the Beast,* were written under the image. Randell scratched his head, the top of his blond buzz-cut hair greasy from lack of washing. We were at an age when we were all discovering the value of personal hygiene. But Randell prided himself on not giving in to peer pressure on the issue of showering. He looked down and shrugged his shoulders. "Nothing."

"It was a white powder," said Shannon. "I saw him put it in her drink."

"It was just sugar," said Randell. "It wasn't poison, just regular sugar."

"Do you think that's funny?" Mrs. Sanders glared at him. "Well, do you?"

"No," said Randell as he looked down at his desk.

"People are dying of cyanide poisoning, and you think it's some kind of joke?"

Randell sat in silence. After what felt like an eternity, Mrs. Sanders told Amy to dump out her cup and then return to her seat.

Shannon raised her hand.

"What is it, Shannon?"

"Mrs. Sanders, what's happening in Chicago?"

"You mean with the murders?" asked Amy.

"Right," said Shannon. "Someone is putting poison in Tylenol."

My stomach tightened. The image of the murdered woman I found when I was five flashed into my awareness.

"Like the way Randell put the white powder in my drink," said Amy.

"Shut up," said Randell. "I didn't mean anything by it."

"Watch it, Randell," said Mrs. Sanders.

Randell lowered his eyes. He focused on scribbling a picture of *Eddie* in his notebook with his pencil.

"Well," said Mrs. Sanders, "I'm not an expert, but I do watch the news. Yes, someone has been killing people by putting cyanide in over-the-counter medicine capsules. So, the police are hunting for the killer, and they are pulling Tylenol from store shelves."

"Oh no," said Max, a heavy-set boy with blond hair. "I took one a few days ago." Max's eyes were wide with terror. "Mrs. Sanders, I have to go to the nurse's office. Now!"

"You're fine," said our teacher. "If the one you took had cyanide in it, you'd be dead like *that*—" She snapped her fingers. "Just don't take anymore until they find the killer."

"I heard police were driving through the streets using loudspeakers. They're warning people to throw out their Tylenol," said Shannon. "Or to return it, or something."

"That's right," said Mrs. Sanders. "And all around the country, people are flooding hospitals by the thousands. They are afraid they have been poisoned. Like Max, they took the medicine, and now they're terrified."

"How many have been killed?" asked Amy.

"Seven people so far," I said.

Mrs. Sanders nodded and sat behind her desk. "And after the first wave of murders, they found a second batch of Tylenol laced with cyanide. Johnson & Johnson are intensifying their recall."

"Good," I said. "That's the right thing to do."

Mrs. Sanders nodded. "It's the largest recall ever of medicine of any kind."

"And I heard they were offering a reward," said Shannon.

"Yes, one hundred thousand dollars."

"Wow," said Max. "I wish I knew something."

"Do they know who the killer is?" asked Amy. She ran her fingers through her hair.

"No," said our teacher. "But hundreds of police and FBI agents are working on it."

"I hope they catch him," said Amy.

"Mrs. Sanders, why would someone do something like this?" I asked.

"Who knows?" asked Mrs. Sanders. "Some people do crazy things. No one knows why."

"I guess so," I said, feeling sad for the victims and their families. "But I'd like to understand why people do bad things. There must be something wrong with the way their brain works. And I want to know why God lets them."

Mrs. Sanders smiled. "Maybe you'll be a psychologist one day. Or a theologian. But enough philosophy for today. Class, take out your math books and turn to page 105."

The sound of pages turning filled the classroom. Sitting in silence for a moment, I thought about all that was happening in our world. After a moment, I sighed, opened my math book, and turned to the proper page. I had a hard time concentrating on my assignment that day. I wasn't a fan of math anyway, and my mind was filled with bigger questions. I wanted to know the meaning behind the murders. And I found Mrs. Sanders answers unsatisfying.

***

After school, I walked to the bus. As I reached the door to the bus, I heard a horn honking. My friend Dan was sitting nearby in his old beat-up Datsun B210.

"Want a ride home?" he called.

"Sure!" I said. I ran over to Dan's green car. A smile spread across my face as I ran. I was thrilled to not have to endure the hour and a half bus ride to take me the grand distance of three miles to my home.

"Thanks, Dan," I called through the open window. I opened the front door and threw my brown leather knapsack into the back. There was a Stephen King novel sitting on the passenger seat. I picked it up and sat on the weathered upholstery.

"What's this?" I turned the book over in my hands. I read the title aloud, "The Gunslinger."

"Yeah, it's good. It's brand new." Dan took a sip from a can of cola sitting in his cup holder. "Just published three months ago."

"What's it about?"

"It's about a man who is a cross between a western gunslinger and a knight. It blends fantasy and horror with westerns."

"Sounds cool."

"Yeah," said Dan. "He's chasing a mysterious figure called 'the man in black.'"

"I assume the gunslinger is the hero of the novel." I flipped the book over and read the back cover.

"Yeah, he's a good guy. He has honor. He remembers the face of his father. And he is on a quest to find The Dark Tower."

"That sounds awesome. What does the Dark Tower symbolize?"

"What do you mean?"

"You know, like does it represent the search for meaning? Or something like that?"

"I don't know," said Dan. "I just like the story."

Dan started his car, and the exhaust backfired. When the road was clear, we pulled out and headed towards my home.

"Did you see the news last night?" asked Dan.

"Yeah," I said as we rode over the country roads. "It was all about the cyanide murders."

"I kind of wish we were in Chicago," said Dan. "I'd like to investigate the murders. If we put our heads together, I bet we could solve the case."

"Me too," I said.

"Maybe we should drive up there," Dan mused.

"Sounds exciting," I said. "But they are working hard on the case. They know what they're doing."

Dan nodded. "They would probably have it solved before we even got there, anyway."

"Yeah."

The car groaned as it struggled to get over the next hill. The wind from the open windows filled the interior with a dull roar. As we crested the hill, the autumn sun danced across the dashboard through the unwashed windshield. The engine purred as we went down the hill, released from its heavy burden.

"Have you ever known a murderer?"

My mind flashed to the murdered woman I found in the hole in Kansas City, years before.

"I don't think so," I said. "Have you?"

"No," said Dan. "But I'd like to be a cop. I'd like to help people. Solve mysteries. Stuff like that. After I graduate, I'm going to join the army."

"To be a cop?"

"Yeah," said Dan. "Well, to be Military Police." He glanced at me and shrugged. "You got to start somewhere."

We pulled into my driveway, and our dogs began barking. I grabbed my knapsack from the back seat.

"See you tomorrow," I said and shut the door.

"See you tomorrow," Dan said through the open window and drove off.

After storing my knapsack, I went out to our barn and put on my boxing gloves. We had a heavy bag there, and next to it was a speed bag. I began my workout with the heavy bag. Dancing around the bag, I worked on my footwork and jabs. After twenty minutes, I turned to the speed bag. I had developed a good rhythm through lots of practice, and spent the next fifteen minutes on the speed bag. When I finished, I lifted my boxing gloves to my teeth and pulled the laces, untying them. Taking off my gloves, I spied my jump rope. Our coach had told us to jump rope to practice footwork, so I spent another fifteen minutes jumping rope.

After that, I climbed aboard our blue tractor and started it. It barked to life and puffed smoke from its exhaust. Adjusting the hand throttle, I drove the tractor to an area of our property we were clearing. I started brush hogging the side area near our southern field. I loved driving our tractor. There was something about the roar of its engine that was soothing to me. I loved seeing the results of my work so fast. After just a few rounds on the tractor, I already had a sense of accomplishment. After working for about an hour, the job was done. I shut the engine off and surveyed my work. The smell of the fresh-cut grass filled the air and brought a smile to my face. I felt good about the job and walked back to our house. Mowing the field made me feel centered and at peace. *God is in Heaven,* I thought, *and all is right with the world.*

"Thanks for mowing the field," said Dad.

"My pleasure," I said, and I meant it. "News time?"

"It's just about to start."

The news opened with images of Tylenol being removed from store shelves. Along with the images, there was a voice-over.

"Breaking news. There has been a big change in the cyanide murder case. Authorities have confirmed they have received an extortion letter."

"Oh wow," said Mom. "I'm glad we are watching tonight."

The news report continued. *"Police have been frantically searching for any information that would lead to finding the killer. The recent extortion letter may be the clue they have been searching for."*

"Extortion," said Dad. "That makes sense."

"A letter demanding $1 million was sent to McNeil Consumer Products Co., the makers of Tylenol, in order to stop the killings. The handwritten letter also serves as a confession of having committed the previous murders in this case."

"Wow," said Mom. "If they catch the guy who wrote the letter, it should be an open and shut case."

"The extortion letter reads as follows ..."

As the newscaster continued, a montage of images flashed across the screen. Pictures of people going into hospitals showed in the background. Police cars with loudspeakers drove through the city warning residents. A woman was holding a crying child, rocking her gently to soothe her.

"Gentlemen," the reporter read from the extortion letter, *"As you can see, it is easy to place cyanide (both potassium and sodium) into capsules sitting on store shelves. And since the cyanide is inside the gelatin, it is easy to get buyers to swallow the bitter pill. Another beauty is that cyanide operates quickly. It takes so very little. And there will be no time to take counter measures. If you don't mind the publicity of these little capsules, then do nothing. So far, I have spent less than fifty dollars. And it takes me less than 10 minutes per bottle. If you want to stop the killing then wire $1*

million to bank account 84-49-597 at Continental Illinois Bank, Chicago, Illinois. Don't attempt to involve the FBI or local Chicago authorities with this letter. A couple of phone calls by me will undo anything you can possibly do."

"Well," said Mom. "This is good news."

"Yes," said Dad. "With a signed confession and threats of future murders, the police will have the killer brought to justice in no time." He looked at me and smiled. "A piece of cake."

I wish I could say Dad was right. I wanted the murderer to be caught and the killings and terror to be over. But the handwritten letter confessing to the crimes and threatening to kill others was only the beginning. Convicting a suspect in this case would prove harder than any of us imagined.

God was still in Heaven, but all was not right with the world.

14
THE GHOST IN THE GLASS

The church bell rang, and we all rose from our seats. Our little church barely held thirty people, but on that day, every seat was filled. It was what the diocese called a "chicken coop," a small mission church in a little country town. But since the murders started, attendance had swelled to capacity. The faint hint of incense haunted the air as we began the service.

    Glancing back, I saw Father Andrew, our priest. He was clothed in a green chasable and stole. His short white hair was neatly combed to the side, and his silver glasses framed his clean-shaven face. He nodded at the organist, Mrs. O'Kelly. Her pink dress and matching hat were placed to perfection, but her large-framed glasses rode low on her nose. She nodded to the priest, pushed her glasses back with her left hand, and made the sign of the cross with her right. She then smiled, laid her fingers on the organ's keyboard, and started playing the wrong hymn. Realizing her mistake, Mrs. O'Kelly stopped playing; she waved her hands like she was wiping clean the error. She adjusted her glasses and tried again.

As the opening hymn played on the old organ, Father Andrew entered the nave from the back of the church and processed to the front. He paused for a moment, bowed at the altar, and then continued to his place. When the music was over, he began the liturgy. After the opening prayers and Scripture readings, Father Andrew read the Gospel assigned for that day. After he finished, we all sat. Father Andrew stood at the pulpit and gazed out at the congregation.

"Good morning, everyone."

"Good morning," we all mumbled, somewhat in unison.

"I'm going to preach on the readings for today, but first I want to share something with you. What I have to say is important during this difficult time." Father Andrew cleared his throat. "So anyway, I'm just going to speak to you from my heart."

My brother Ed yawned. Becky colored a picture of Adam and Eve in the Garden of Eden. She only had one short, broken, yellow crayon, and so the first couple looked a little jaundiced. Slouching in my seat, I watched her fill in the black and white outlines of the picture.

"We all are glued to our television sets these days," he continued. "We watch the evening news like it was a murder mystery movie. We discuss the killings everywhere we go. But what is happening in our world is *not* fiction. It's all too real. My friends, I want to talk this morning about the cyanide murders, and the fear that is gripping our country right now. I want to talk to you about the problem of evil."

This sounded much more interesting than Father Andrew's last sermon about the importance of constancy. I sat up straight and listened.

"Let me be blunt," he continued. "Someone is committing a terrible evil in the Chicago area. And this evil is rippling out across this great land. Copycat criminals are following in the unknown killer's footsteps. The last I heard, there've been over two hundred copycat incidents. Good people are dead. Americans are terrified. And we struggle to make sense of the madness."

I glanced around at the congregation. Everyone's attention was glued to Father Andrew.

"We're people of faith. We're not perfect, but we try to do our best. We believe in a good God. A God who is all-powerful and present everywhere. A God who loves us and wants the best for us. A God who sees all and knows all."

Becky held up the picture she had colored for me to see. I smiled and nodded, then turned my attention back to the sermon.

"So, if God is all-powerful, all-knowing, and all-good," Father Andrew paused and looked around the church, "why is there evil in the world? Why do bad things happen to good people? Why did someone put cyanide poison into a safe and popular painkiller? Why did they murder all those innocent people?"

Silence hung in the air. A little boy named Billy, his dark hair greased and slicked back, noticed the heavy silence. "Uh-oh," he said. The congregation laughed, easing the tension. Father Andrew looked at Billy and smiled. Billy's eyes brightened and he tried his unintentional joke again, this time with great gusto. "Uh-oh!" But the second time around, there was little response. Billy shrugged and turned his attention back to playing with a toy car.

"Throughout history, many answers have been given. Some say human suffering is divine retribution for personal sins. But I reject that idea. That doesn't fit with the God of our faith." He cleared his throat. "Others say God Himself causes the evil to occur. They say He does this to work out a divine plan for His glory. But I reject that idea, too. Again, it just doesn't sound like the God revealed in Scripture, reason, and tradition."

The congregation seemed puzzled. Father Andrew read the crowd and pushed ahead to his main point.

"So, how do we make sense of evil? Why is there suffering? If God is good, why is there so much bad in the world? Today, we are going to focus on one of many possible solutions to these questions."

Someone whispered behind me. I glanced back and saw Mr. Jennings talking to his wife. She held her finger to her lips, suggesting for him to be quiet and listen.

"My friends," Father Andrew continued, "God has given us both free will and ethical instruction. He has given us moral principles to follow and the free will to either follow them or reject them. We can choose to follow God's commandments or not. It's up to us. God doesn't *make* us follow His commandments, but He *wants* us to make the right choice and obey Him."

Mrs. O'Kelly's fingers accidentally hit the keyboard of the organ, making a sudden jumble of notes. "Oh!" she said. She glanced around the church and whispered, "Sorry!"

Father Andrew continued. "God wants us to grow morally and ethically. Also, suffering in this life helps to prepare us for eternal life in Heaven. Although we suffer temporarily, what we gain eternally is immeasurable."

He looked around the room and smiled. "And *that's* the meaning of suffering."

There was a moment of silence. Someone coughed. Father Andrew took a deep breath and let it out.

"Now," he said. "I'm going to preach this morning on our reading from the New Testament ..."

After the service, Father Andrew stood in the back of the church. As people filed out, he shook their hands and wished them to have a good week. When I came to him, Father Andrew smiled.

"How's school going, Jack?"

"It's fine," I said. "No complaints. I thought your sermon today was interesting. Especially the part about the cyanide murders."

"I'm glad you liked it."

"So, your point is that God doesn't want us to be robots, right?"

Father Andrew looked puzzled. "I'm not sure what you mean."

"Well, if God didn't give us free will, we would just be like robots, right? And that's no good. God doesn't want robots." I paused, seeing he wasn't following my analogy. "You know, *robots*. Like C3PO or R2D2. From *Star Wars*."

"I'm afraid I haven't seen it," he smiled.

"You know, a robot," I said. "Danger Will Robinson! Danger!"

"Oh, sure! From *Lost in Space*!"

"Right! Without free will, we would be like robots. We would be programmed to love God and follow his commandments, but we wouldn't develop morally."

"Exactly! Maybe you should have preached the sermon today." Father Andrew smiled again. "Have you ever thought of becoming a priest?"

"I have, but I want to do lots of other things, too."

"Like what?"

"Oh, lots of stuff. I want to be an actor, a writer, maybe work in psychology," I shrugged. "Lots of stuff."

"All of that would be great training for the priesthood."

"Yeah," I said, "and I do feel called to ministry. But I also feel called to marriage and family life."

"Well, maybe God will work it out." Father Andrew smiled. "So," he said, looking me in the eye. "Do you agree with my explanation of evil and suffering?"

"I think it's a good start ..."

"But?"

"But I don't think it's the whole answer."

"Why's that?"

"Well, it's good as far as it goes. It does contain some truth. It hints at part of an answer. I agree that our present struggles give us an opportunity to become better people. Suffering helps us to improve our souls."

"So, we're on the same page."

"Kind of," I said. "God can and does bring good out of bad. But that doesn't mean God causes or allows suffering to make us better people." I shrugged. "It's just a positive side effect."

"Well, yes, but there is also free will involved. Having free choices allows us to develop morally."

"Yeah, I agree. I love the idea of ongoing moral development. But what about the free will of the victims? What about their moral development?

They're not just collateral damage. They matter. What about them?" I glanced at our priest. "I guess I'm skeptical."

"Of the existence of God?"

I shook my head. "No, not of God. Of the ability of a limited human mind to understand the infinite mind of God."

There was a long pause. Fearing I had offended him, I shifted back and forth on my feet. Father Andrew then let out a good-natured laugh and patted me on the back.

"You see!" he said. "You should become a priest!"

***

The following Wednesday, my family and I gathered for our evening meal. Brad had gotten married earlier that year and no longer lived with us. So, at dinner were my parents, Ed, Becky, and me. Mom made fried chicken, along with homemade mashed potatoes and buttered corn on the cob. As great as all of that was, my favorite was the whole-grain, homemade bread, crafted from our homegrown wheat. Hints of fresh-baked bread and hot buttered corn on the cob rode the air from the kitchen into the dining room. The rich scents blended to create a delightful symphony.

"So," said Dad. "Did anything interesting happen today?"

"Toby brought a chicken to school," said Ed. He took a bite of fried chicken.

"A chicken?" said Mom, pouring a glass of sweet tea. "You mean a real chicken?"

"Yeah, a real live chicken," said Ed. He wiped his mouth and took a drink of tea. "He put it in a storage shed at the school."

Dad smiled. "Becky, did anything happen at school today?"

"No." Becky stopped eating her bread and looked up. "Why? What did you hear?"

"We didn't hear anything," said Dad, and chuckled.

"Oh, okay," Becky resumed eating her bread. "Good."

Mom glanced at Dad. "We'll come back to that later."

"How about you, Jack?" asked Dad.

"I had a good day," I said. "I tried out for the school play."

"Oh, great," said Mom as she buttered a piece of bread.

"How'd your audition go?" asked Dad.

"Good. My character is a southern guy, so I played it like Andy Griffith." I smiled. "I got the part."

"That sounds fun," said Mom. "Good job putting yourself out there."

As I buttered an ear of corn, I continued. "Oh, and some of the guys and I talked about why someone would commit the cyanide murders."

"Oh?" said Mom. "Besides extortion, what are the theories?"

"Well, we wondered if maybe competitors could have done it. You know, to make their product more popular."

"That's possible," said Dad.

"We also thought that maybe the killer wanted to only kill one specific person, but he did the random killings to throw police off his trail."

"I wondered that, too," said Mom. "It seems like something a smart murderer might do."

"Maybe revenge was the motive," said Dad.

"We discussed that, too."

"Revenge, extortion, cover-up, they're all possibilities," said Dad.

"Right," I said. "But I also wondered if maybe the killer weirdly thought he was doing a good deed."

"How's that?" asked Mom.

"Well, if the killer was mentally unstable, he might have thought he was alerting the public to a dangerous product. Of course, Tylenol is completely safe. But if someone is unstable, they may think otherwise." I took a bite of the corn and cleaned my face with a cloth napkin. "He may even have thought he was doing a greater good, even though what he did was actually a terrible evil. But in his distorted way of thinking, maybe it all made sense in his twisted logic."

There was a long silence. After a few moments, metal forks clicked against ceramic plates again.

I took a bite of hot buttered bread. I looked up at Mom. "Did anything exciting happen here?"

"Not really," said Mom. "Nothing exciting ever happens here." She smiled. "We worked on some things. The goats got out again." She took a bite of mashed potatoes. "Are you going to watch the news with us again tonight?"

"Yeah," I said. "I want to see what's happening with the case."

We finished dinner, and Ed and I washed the dishes. Afterward, my parents and I gathered for what had become our evening ritual. We sat in front of the television to watch the national news. Every day, we hoped for a break in the cyanide murder case. As usual, the news led with information about the murders.

"In an important step forward in solving the cyanide murders, police have released a headshot of the prime suspect."

"Oh wow," said Mom. "I'm glad we're watching tonight."

"Me too," I added.

"Listen," said Dad. He turned up the volume.

The news report continued: *"Police have tracked the writer of the extortion letter to a man named Robert Richardson."*

"Yes!" I said, squeezing my hand into a fist of triumph. "They'll get him in no time now."

The news showed an image of a white, middle-aged man with glasses and a beard.

"Oh, my goodness," said my mother as she stood up. She walked forward and stared at the screen, her left hand covering her mouth. Mom pointed at the headshot of the prime suspect on the television.

"That's John Price!"

15
DEAD HUNT

"It can't be John Price," said my father. "The news said his name is Robert Richardson."

"Harry, come on!" said Mom. "I'd know that face anywhere."

"But John doesn't live in Chicago."

"We don't know where he lives now," said my mother.

Suddenly the room was hot, even though it was October. In the background, the newscaster continued. *"If you know the whereabouts of Robert Richardson, please call the police hotline dedicated to this case ..."*

"I thought they lived in Kansas City," I said. "He and Sarah manage our houses there."

"Oh, not anymore," said Mom, her eyes wide. "One of our houses was in dispute, and it led to the end of our business relationship with them."

"What happened?"

"The people renting-to-own the house filed for bankruptcy. John was supposed to represent us at the hearing, but he never showed up. We ended up losing the house."

"We tried to find out what happened to him," said Dad, "but we were just told he left the state. Sarah too. Gone."

"And they have our important papers with them," said Mom. "They took care of everything, so they had everything."

Dad looked at Mom and winced. "Even our social security numbers."

"Why did they have your social security numbers?"

"Well, they called and asked for them," said Mom. She took a deep breath. "They said they needed them. This was a while back."

Dad looked calm. "This is very common in business. We were a little surprised when they asked for them, but they have a way of convincing people about things."

"Right," said Mom. "I've never seen John angry. He always is eerily calm."

"Yeah, and Sarah is so professional," said Dad. "And John is one of the smartest people I've ever met."

I paced back and forth across the living room. 'So, after they skipped out on the hearing, maybe they went to Chicago."

"Maybe," said Dad. "But we still don't know for sure if that picture was really of him."

"It was," said Mom. "His mouth and eyes are very distinctive. I always thought they looked cruel." She paused and seemed lost in thought.

"Listen," I said as another face flashed up on the glass of the television screen. I turned the volume up.

"Something about his eyes," said Mom, and shook her head.

"Right," said Dad. "His eyes and mouth, especially after his daughter—"

"Listen!"

The news showed an image of a woman in glasses. *"... is a photo of Nancy Richardson, Robert Richardson's wife ..."*

"That's Sarah!" said Mom.

Excitement filled me as I realized we could help solve this case. It was the biggest unsolved murder mystery of our time, and we could do something to stop it. We could help bring a killer to justice.

"It can't be them," said Dad. "It just can't be!"

"Harry, look at them," said Mom. "That's them!"

"It must be a coincidence," he said. "We can't be sure. We need more information."

"We need to tell someone!" I shouted.

There was a long silence. Television commercials flickered in the background.

Finally, Mom said, "No, your father's right. We don't have enough evidence at this point. Maybe they just look like John and Sarah, that's all."

"Middle-aged white male," said Dad, and shrugged.

"Like most serial killers," I added.

Dad thought for a moment and then he shook his head. "We just can't be sure. We don't want to derail the police investigation with a random observation. Not at this point. We need to know for sure first."

My cheeks felt hot. "But you could call the tip hotline for the case that the news mentioned."

"Jack, I don't want to get them in trouble if we don't have to."

"I agree," said Mom. "For now, this is for the best."

Picking up a comic book from the coffee table, I stood and paced the living room. I rolled the comic into a cylinder and tapped it against my palm. My mind rushed back to the flashlight John had given me years before when I was five years old and so very sick. After drinking the soda. After finding the murdered woman. *Tap, tap, tap. Tap, tap, tap.*

"Don't worry," said Dad. "If they have a better photo that's more clearly him, we'll call."

I looked at him but said nothing.

"I promise," he added.

I tapped the rolled comic in my hands. "The kids at school are going to be interested in all this."

Mom glanced at Dad. "Jack," she said, "don't tell the kids at school that you think it's John Price in the police headshot."

"Why not?"

"This is a serious situation. An unknown serial killer is terrifying the nation. People are dying. Copycat killers are coming out of the woodwork. We don't want anyone to think we're connected to the murderer."

"Which we're not," said Dad.

"Right," said Mom. "Which we're not."

"Of course not," I said.

"But we're still new here. People don't know us that well. It takes a long time in rural areas for people to fully accept you as one of their own." Mom paused. "We're still thought of as outsiders. We don't want a misunderstanding to create trouble for us."

"Besides," said Dad. "It probably isn't John."

"Right," said Mom. "Just keep quiet about it for now. Don't tell anyone."

"What if it turns out to be him?" I asked.

"If it turns out to be him," added Mom, "we'll cooperate with the investigation in every way possible. If they want, we'll talk to the FBI."

"But not the kids at school," said Dad. He looked me in the eye. "We'll tell the FBI everything. We'll do whatever we can to help. But don't tell your classmates. This is an open case. It could make it harder for the police if it goes public too soon."

As I thought, I ran my fingers through my hair. "I did read that sometimes the police withhold certain facts from the public," I said. "They do it to help determine if the suspects are guilty. If a person of interest knows information that hasn't been made public, it means they may be involved with the crime."

"Right," said Mom. "So, don't tell the kids at school. Keep it quiet for now. Got it?"

Disappointment crept over me. We had a chance to help solve the crime of the century, but I had to play it cool. I glanced at the rolled-up comic book in my hand. *Like a superhero keeping his identity a secret.* I looked at my parents and nodded.

"Got it."

***

The next day, Dan came to my house after school, and we were sighting in my rifle. My father had given me a .22 caliber rifle for my fourteenth birthday. My brothers and I were into sport shooting that year. We liked to compete against ourselves and each other in friendly contests of accuracy. So, Dan and I set up a target and shooting range in my back pasture. We braced my rifle on a table so it wouldn't move and took turns shooting it at the target. Each time we shot, we adjusted the sights just a little to make them as precise as possible. After twenty minutes of work, we were getting pretty accurate.

Bang!

"That's pretty close to the center," said Dan, looking through his binoculars. "I think we should move the site just a hair to the left."

Adjusting the sights slightly to the left, I looked up at Dan. "Let's try it again. Stand back." I aimed. "Ready?"

"Ready."

Looking through the sites at the bullseye, I squeezed the trigger.

Bang!

Dan looked through his binoculars again. "Man, that's real close to perfect."

"Can I use your binocs?" I asked. He nodded and handed them to me. I looked through them at the target. "Yeah, that's right on the money."

"Let's try some free shooting," said Dan.

I reloaded my rifle and handed it to him.

Bang! Bang! Bang!

Looking through the binoculars, I saw his three shots were very close to the center. I shot the next three with similar accuracy. *Bang! Bang! Bang!*

"That looks good to me," said Dan.

"Me too. I think we got it sighted in."

"Yeah," said Dan. "It was kind of fun." He smiled.

We picked up the spent shells and started walking back towards Dan's car.

"Did you see the guy on the news they think is the Tylenol killer?" asked Dan. "His name is

Richardson. He's from Texas, I think. Somewhere like that."

"I saw the guy," I said. My stomach tightened. "Maybe that's his name, maybe not."

"You mean maybe he's using an alias?"

"Right," I said. "His real name could be anything."

"That's a good point."

"It'd be fun to be a detective," he said. "Solve crimes. Catch killers."

"Yeah, it would be a good way of helping people."

As we walked, the dried leaves of late autumn crunched beneath our boots.

"Now that he's on the run," said Dan, "it will be interesting to see if the killings stop."

"I certainly hope they do," I said. "There's already been too many."

"Yeah."

"But I know what you're saying. If the killings stop while he's on the run, it's more proof he did it."

"Exactly."

We sat under a bare oak tree near Dan's Datsun. I opened my gun cleaning kit and worked on my rifle. Dan held a well-worn paperback book in his hands.

"What's that book?"

"Dune," said Dan, a grin spreading across his face. "It's by Frank Herbert."

"I always wanted to read that," I said, putting oil on my rifle. "I heard it's a blend of science fiction, political intrigue, and mysticism."

"Yeah, it's cool."

Dan handed me the book and I thumbed through its pages. I stopped at random and read aloud: *"Fear is the mind-killer."* I looked at Dan. "Wow."

Dan nodded. "It's from the 'The Litany Against Fear.'"

I handed the book back to him. "Maybe I can borrow that when you're finished."

"Absolutely.'

As I cleaned my rifle, Dan talked about his plans for after high school. He was two years older than me and excited about his future.

"I want to do something exciting after I graduate," he said. "I want to have an adventure."

Running a white cotton patch coated with oil down the barrel of my rifle, I nodded. "I love a good adventure."

"Right," said Dan. "I'm looking forward to getting out there into the world. I want to travel, go to Europe, all kinds of stuff."

"So, your ticket there will be joining the army and becoming an MP?"

"Yeah," he smiled. "I've been reading a lot about it. It should be fun. I read a great novel about World War II." He paused, and then added, "You should join, too. They have a buddy program."

"Serving your country is a great thing. I'm glad you found what you want to do," I said, wiping the oil from my rifle with an old brown cloth. "But it's not for me."

"Why not?"

"Their commercial says they do more before 9 a.m. than most people do all day." I smiled. "That sounds awful!"

Dan laughed. "Yeah, well, that is not their strongest selling point."

"Besides, I'm a pacifist." I grinned. "That might hurt a long-term career in the military."

Dan laughed. "Yeah, maybe you're right."

I put my gun cleaning kit back together and stood up. "But I hope you find the adventure you're looking for."

"Thanks," said Dan.

My parents came out onto our porch and waved. Mom's face looked serious.

"Hi there, Dan," called my father.

"Hello, Mr. and Mrs. Kerrigan," he said. "Beautiful Fall afternoon."

"I'll say it is," said Dad.

Dan turned to me. "It looks like they want to talk to you about something. I'd better go."

Nodding, I said, "I think you're right. See you later."

Dan started his car, and black smoke shot out of the tailpipe. He looked at me and grinned. "Just seven more easy payments and she's all mine!"

Laughing, I waved goodbye. Dan drove down our driveway, and his exhaust backfired. He put his arm out his open window and waved.

My parents walked over to talk to me.

"Is everything okay?" I asked.

"Yes," said Dad. "Interesting news."

"There was a big break in the case," said Mom.

Anticipation crept over me. "What happened?"

"Well, after the FBI released the headshot of the writer of the extortion letter—"

"The one they called Robert Richardson," added Dad.

"I remember."

"Right," said Mom. "After that, the Kansas City police saw the picture."

"Oh, wow."

Dad nodded his head. "They recognized him. He was someone they had arrested before on murder charges." Dad glanced at my mother.

"His name wasn't Robert Richardson," said Mom.

"Jack, your mother was right. It really is John Price."

My hands felt cold and pins and needles ran up my arms.

"Wow," I said. "Are they sure?"

Mom's piercing blue eyes were wide. She stood in the October sun; her face was tight with concern.

"They're positive."

16
ARMED AND DANGEROUS

My brother Brad and I rode in his white Chevy Blazer over the dusty roads. Brad was twenty years old that year, and I was six years younger. The mid-October light filtered through the bare trees, casting shadows over the dirt road. Dad wanted us to practice with our revolvers in a safe environment. As Brad and I neared the shooting range, the radio newscast gave us an update of the hunt for the prime suspect in the cyanide murders. " ... *the FBI is leaving no stone unturned in a nationwide manhunt for John and Sarah Price, wanted in connection to the Chicago Tylenol Murders. Please remember they should be considered armed and dangerous. Now back to today's featured artist, Jerry Reed.*" The song *Amos Moses* came to life on the radio, and Brad turned the volume down.

"You prefer rock music," said Brad. "Right?"

"Yeah. Rock and roll." I smiled. "The 'and roll' part is important."

"Yeah, I guess you're right." Brad took off his sunglasses and hung them from the visor. "I'm into country."

"Jerry Reed is sort of in-between."

"Yeah, I guess so." Brad's green flannel shirt hung down over his belt, and his brown beard framed his face. A grey trucker's cap tilted far back on his head. "Does Dad think the Prices will come to your place?"

"He thinks they might," I said. "When John visited us before, he mentioned something that got Dad worried."

"What did he say?"

"He looked out towards our forest and said a man could hide out there forever."

"That's not good," said Brad. He was quiet for a moment. "So, what's Dad doing for security?"

"Well, he put guns at each door, along with a few hand weapons."

"Like what?"

"Oh, you know, baseball bats, my nunchucks, stuff like that."

"That's good," said Brad. "You can't be too careful."

We hit a bump in the road, jostling the cab. We laughed as we turned off the dirt road into the parking lot of the shooting range. Scanning the parking lot, I saw we were alone.

Brad turned off the engine and looked at me. "Is that why Dad gave you the revolver? In case John shows up?"

"Yeah, he said he knows I like to walk a lot, so I should always take this with me," I patted the .22 caliber revolver in my brown leather holster on my right hip. "Well, just until they catch John, that is."

The Chevy Blazer sat high above the ground, and I had to jump down when I got out of the vehicle. Brad collected guns, and he had bought a brand new .44 Magnum a few weeks earlier. He brought his new handgun and a box of bullets with us and we walked over to the quiet shooting range.

Brad put in his earplugs. "That .22 is a great choice," he said. "The bullets are cheap, and you can shoot it a ton and get good with it." He held up the box of .44 Magnum bullets. "These are expensive. About fifty cents a shot."

Putting in my earplugs, I nodded my head. As we loaded our handguns, Brad looked over at me.

"Ready?"

I tucked my black t-shirt into my blue jeans. "Fire at will."

Brad fired six shots in rapid succession, and the smell of gunpowder filled the air. As he unloaded, I stepped forward into the staging area.

"Ready?" I asked.

He nodded. "Let 'er rip."

As I removed my revolver from my holster, I checked the safety. Moving it to the red "Fire" position, I aimed at the target. Then I shot six times at the target next to his, with similar accuracy. My revolver didn't kick at all, but the same smell of gunpowder rode the autumn breeze.

"Nice."

"Thanks."

"Jack, if someone tried to hurt the family, do you think you could stop them?"

After making sure my revolver was empty, I put the safety on and returned it to my holster. "I hope so."

Brad squinted into the afternoon light. "You may have to. There comes a time in every man's life when he has had to grow up and do hard things." He reloaded his revolver. "It's no fun, but life requires it."

Brushing the dried brown leaves off the shooting table, I nodded. "Yeah, I know."

"People are terrified right now," said Brad. "The Chicago Tylenol killer has the nation in a panic."

"And we know the prime suspect."

"Right."

I shook my head. "I hope this craziness ends soon."

"Me too." Brad stopped working on his revolver and looked at me. "Are you scared?"

"I'm not scared at all." I shrugged. "If anything, I'm excited. It's an adventure. And maybe we can help."

"You're a fourteen-year-old boy," said Brad, and smiled. "Excitement is normal."

"But I hope they catch the killer fast."

"Me too." Brad handed his loaded .44 Magnum to me. "Here you go. Want to give it a shot?"

"Sure." I looked down at the shiny black metal and felt the weight of the weapon in my hands.

"Do you like it?"

"I admire the craftsmanship," I said. "But if I could wave a magic wand and make all the guns in the world disappear, I would."

Brad nodded. "It will kick more than your .22," said Brad, "but the heavy frame will help absorb it."

Aiming at the target, I squeezed my hand around the trigger and pulled. The revolver kicked in my hands and the gun barrel climbed a couple of inches in the air. I paused and glanced at my big brother. Brad smiled and nodded; I fired the last five rounds into the target.

"That's good," said Brad.

I opened the cylinder and kicked out the spent brass shells. "Thanks."

We took out our earplugs. "You're an excellent shot. You've got good shooting skills. But I hope you never have to use them." He smiled again.

Turning the empty revolver around and handing it to Brad, I nodded my head.

"Me too."

***

THE PAIN KILLER

It was already dark that evening when I went to rehearsal for the school play. The students arrived one by one. *In the Air Tonight* by Phil Collins was playing on the radio in our classroom. We chatted about the movie *E.T.* as we waited for the whole group to arrive. When the last student walked in the door, our drama coach, Mr. Simmons, called the group together. We began with theatre games to get warmed up and ready to perform. First, we did vocal exercises followed by stretches, and then improv acting scenes. Mr. Simmons put one-sentence improv ideas into an old bowler hat. We divided up into groups of two actors and drew the performance prompts from the hat. We then performed the scenes with no prior rehearsal, making up the lines and movements as we would go. It was one of my favorite drama club activities.

My partner that night for improv was Jessica Bell. Mr. Simmons said we would go first. Jessica reached into the hat and pulled out a slip of paper. It read: *I think I'm feeling sick*. She pulled her brunette hair back into a ponytail and put on a pair of oversized prop glasses. Since we were allowed to use a table and two chairs, we set the scene at a fancy restaurant. After exchanging a few general ideas with each other, we were ready to begin our improv scene for the class. Our idea for the scene was simple—we pretended all was going well during a rare dinner away at an expensive place. The class was laughing with us as we rolled through our improvised dialogue. Then we came to the main idea of the sketch.

"This is great," said Jessica, pretending to drink a glass of expensive champagne. "This is so yummy! Ah, a perfect evening. Nothing could spoil it. Nothing!"

"Yeah, a perfect evening," my character said. "Absolutely perfect. Nothing could—" I stopped speaking and stood up.

"What's wrong, dear?" asked Jessica's character.

"Uh oh." I grabbed my stomach and twisted my face into a comical grimace.

"Too much asparagus?"

"I think I'm feeling sick!"

"Oh, no!" said Jessica, leaping up. "Did you take Tylenol?"

"Cut!" said Mr. Simmons. "Stop the scene." He clapped his hands, and we stopped acting and looked at our drama coach. His yellow polo shirt and tan slacks were wrinkled from a long day. Mr. Simmons took off his glasses and cleaned them.

"What's wrong?" asked Jessica.

"Jessica, that's not funny," he said. He checked his glasses for smudges. "People are dying. Seven people died in three days. You shouldn't joke about it."

"I heard they also found a guy dead in Wyoming," said a classmate. "They tested him and found he had taken Tylenol laced with cyanide."

"I heard that, too," said someone else. "And the store he got it from gets their supply from a place in Chicago."

"And all the copycat crimes," said Jill, a petite blond with a pierced nose. Jill's mother taught Current Events at the high school. "Acid in make-up, stuff like that."

"Nobody's safe," said Jessica. "Mr. Simmons, I'm scared."

Mr. Simmons put his glasses on. "We're all scared," he said. "It's a terrifying time."

"I'm sorry about the Tylenol joke," said Jessica. "I wasn't thinking."

"It's okay," said Mr. Simmons. "We just need to be respectful."

"Did they catch the guy yet?" asked Jessica.

"No," I said. "He's still on the run."

"His name is John Price," said Mr. Simmons.

"The FBI is doing a nationwide manhunt," I added. "They're looking for him everywhere."

"He's the killer?" asked Bobby, a heavy-set boy wearing a red and white Kansas City Chiefs shirt.

"He's a suspect," I said.

"But he did it?"

"Allegedly," I said.

"He sent a handwritten letter to the company saying he did it," said Jill. "He wrote a confession to the murders in the letter."

"And he threatened to kill more," said someone else.

"I didn't hear about the letter," said Jessica.

Mr. Simmons sat on his desk. "The FBI first thought the letter was a hoax," he said. "But the Kansas City police told them Price was a conman. He was already on the run from the police for other crimes."

Jill paced the floor. "And the police had charged him with murder in another case."

"The murder of Raymond West," I said.

Jill nodded. "That sounds right."

"But why don't they just arrest him?" asked Bobby.

"That's the problem," said Mr. Simmons.

"They can't find him," I said. "He and his wife are on the run from the law."

"There is a police tip hotline people can call," said Jill. "I heard they're receiving hundreds of calls."

"There are reported sightings coming in from all over the country," I said. "It must be hard to sift through them all."

"That's right," said Mr. Simmons. "In Amarillo, Texas, police say the picture of Price looks like the sketch of a jewel thief they are hunting for."

"And there was a report that Price and his wife were at a baseball game," said Jill, rubbing her neck.

"Who was playing?" asked Bobby.

"The St. Louis Cardinals and some other team, I think."

Bobby clapped his hands. "Yeah!" he shouted. "Go Cardinals!"

Mr. Simmons rolled his eyes. "And there have been reported sightings of them just an hour from here."

"Really?" I said. "Where?"

"Over in Carl Junction," said Mr. Simmons. "Near Joplin."

"That's where John Price is from," I said. "He grew up on a farm near there."

"Oh, yeah?" said Mr. Simmons. "How do you know that?"

I looked down at my feet. "I must have heard it somewhere."

"Yeah, well," he said, "they say six people there said they saw him and his wife."

"Oh, wow."

"Yeah," he continued. "One woman reported Price was hiding in an old abandoned house, but it turned out not to be him."

"Was anyone there?" asked Bobby.

"Just someone feeding their pet gophers."

Jessica smiled. "I love gophers. They're so cute!"

"And a hairstylist there said she saw him," said Mr. Simmons. He ran his fingers through his thinning hair, and I noticed for the first time it was dyed. "She said John Price came in and asked to have his hair dyed. But when she talked about the Tylenol murders, he ran out."

"What did she do?" I asked.

"She called the police, and they tracked the guy down," he said. "Turns out he realized he didn't have enough money with him to pay."

"My mom said callers have reported seeing the Price's everywhere from Miami to here in Missouri," said Jill. "And all in the same day."

Bobby smiled. "All I know is if he's a Cardinal's fan, he can't be all bad."

"Don't be an idiot," said Jill. "If they're only an hour away, none of us are safe."

Chills ran up my spine. I couldn't tell if it was fear or excitement. Sometimes it was hard to tell the difference.

A knock came at our classroom door. Mr. Cline, the school janitor, stood in the doorway, his face overcast with thunderclouds.

"They have a new lead in the Chicago Tylenol murders," he said. Mr. Cline took his black cowboy hat off and held it in his hands. "Turn on the news. Quick!"

We had a television set in our classroom, and I ran to it and turned it on. It took forever to warm up, but as it did, Mr. Cline told us a little about what was happening.

"The police released a surveillance camera photo from an ATM," he said. "It was in a drugstore where a victim bought tainted Tylenol."

"So what?" asked Bobby.

"So, they think the killer is in the photo's background," said Mr. Cline, "watching her buy the poisoned medicine."

My hands were cold, and pins and needles ran up my arms. When the old TV finally warmed up, the words SPECIAL REPORT flashed on the screen.

"We interrupt this program to bring you a special report. A drugstore surveillance camera photo has provided a break in the Chicago Tylenol Murders. We have identified the woman buying tainted Tylenol in the photo as Paula Prince."

"That's the poor woman who was the seventh victim," I said.

"That's right," said Mr. Simmons.

The news report continued: *"On the evening of September 29th, Paula Prince purchased Extra-Strength Tylenol at a local Walgreens. Unbeknownst to her, the Tylenol would turn out to be laced with cyanide poison."*

The news showed a grainy, black-and-white photo of Paula Prince in a drugstore, along with other shoppers.

"This is so sad," said Jessica.

"I know," I said. "My heart goes out to her family."

"Listen," said Mr. Simmons, and turned up the volume.

"Authorities have also noticed a person of interest in the photo. He is in the background, watching Ms. Prince as she makes her fateful purchase. The suspicious man is wearing a light jacket and has a beard. If you have any

information involving the case, police have set up a tip hotline ..."

As the newscaster continued, the camera focused on the mysterious figure in the background.

"Oh, my goodness," said Mr. Simmons. He pointed at the grainy image on the television screen. "That's John Price!"

"Yes," said Jill. "That's the guy!"

"It looks like John to me, too," I said, staring at the television, "but I can't be sure."

"You called him 'John,'" said Jessica, looking at me out of the corner of her eye. "Sounds like you're on a first-name basis."

"Well," I said, "it's just shorthand for his full name."

"What if he really is only an hour away?" said Jill. "Mr. Simmons, what should we do?"

"We have to be careful," said Mr. Simmons, shaking his head. "I'm canceling rehearsal tonight. Go home and be with your families. If he's in Carl Junction, we'll be fine."

"But what if there was something to draw him here to our town?" asked Jill.

My stomach tightened. "My sister ..." I mumbled. Then I remembered she was safe at home. Our parents warned us John and Sarah may come to the school to try to get us. They told us if they did, not to go with them. Mom assured us that no matter what they say or how persuasive they are, she would never have John and Sarah come for us. But she told us to be on guard just in case.

Jessica looked at me. Her brow furrowed as she clenched her hands together. "Oh, no."

"What's wrong?" I asked.

Jessica swallowed hard and looked around at all of us in the room.

"He could be waiting outside in the parking lot right now."

17
HAPPY HALLOWEEN

Usually, during late October, my friends and I would make plans for Halloween. Costumes were always a big part of our conversations. Some of us would dress scary, others preferred funny costumes, and superheroes were always popular. It was always a wonderful time of year. There were haunted houses to visit, themed parties to go to, and candy to hand out to children.

But 1982 was different. Everything had changed. Plans were canceled. Many stayed home. Most houses didn't give out sweet treats or edible goodies. People were afraid. The killer could easily poison candy, just like he did with Extra Strength Tylenol. Even easier. Some neighborhoods canceled Halloween entirely.

Always resilient, Americans adapted fast to the problem. Some gave out small toys instead of candy. Others gave money. Balloons and other fun non-foods were purchased. Even so, many such homes which had creatively planned ahead had few trick-

or-treaters. People stayed home. They were terrified of the Pain Killer.

Meanwhile, John and Sarah Price were on the run. No one knew where they were. Law enforcement personnel, both local and Federal, were searching everywhere for them. Police interviewed clerks from the drug stores where the tainted Extra Strength Tylenol was bought. They tried diligently to find fingerprints, but only a single smudge was obtained from one bottle; it yielded no meaningful results. Law enforcement officers even took police sketches door to door hoping to find any lead that would help. During this process, the FBI went through the Price's client list one by one. They interviewed client after client. And then they came to the names of my parents: Harold and Betty Kerrigan.

One day, after returning home from school, my mother greeted me at the door.

"The FBI was here today," she said.

A strange feeling ran through me. It was a mixture of excitement and concern. "What did they want?"

"They were looking for John and Sarah."

My mother held her hands together and pressed on her palms. Her fingers fidgeted as she looked at me.

"Are you okay?" I asked.

"I'm okay," she said. "I'm just worried. I'm so afraid John and Sarah are going to come for you kids."

"Don't worry, Mom. We're big now."

"I know," she said. "But I'm especially afraid they will try to take Becky. She's still little. And they wanted to have her before. They came right out and asked for us to give her to them." Tears swelled in my mother's eyes.

I patted her on the arm. "Let's go inside."

We went inside our home and sat in the living room. My father was there. Leaning against the wall next to his seat was his 12-gauge shotgun. The shotgun was a single shot model in the "break open" style, and it was resting in the open position. A box of shotgun shells sat nearby. The gun wasn't loaded, but it could be. Fast.

"Dad, what happened?"

Dad smiled. "Oh, nothing much," he said. "Nothing to worry about."

"Mom said the FBI was here looking for John."

"Yeah," said Dad. "They're doing their job well. Trying to catch a killer. Trying to put an end to the madness."

My eyes returned to the shiny black barrel of his 12-gauge. "What's the shotgun for?"

"Oh, just in case."

"In case of what?"

Dad looked me in the eye. "In case John comes by."

Nodding, I rubbed the back of my neck with my hand. "Does the FBI expect him to come here?"

"They think he might," said Dad.

"Do you think so, too?"

Dad was silent for a moment. He glanced at his shotgun. "Yes."

"Jack, no one knows," said Mom. "He's on the run. Some have reported seeing him about an hour from here."

"So, it's possible."

"Right," said Dad. "It's possible."

"Harry, what are we going to do if he comes by?" said Mom.

"Oh, don't worry," said Dad. "He wouldn't hurt us." His smile was unconvincing.

"That's probably what Raymond West thought," said Mom. "Look what happened to him."

Dad nodded his head. "Jack, be careful on your walks."

Mom looked at me. "Maybe you should stay close to home until all this is over."

"I can't," I said. "I love walking. I need to walk to relax and think."

"I know," said Mom. "But this is serious. Stay close."

"Oh, I don't think that's necessary, Betty," said Dad. He turned to me and smiled. "Just be careful. And always take your revolver with you when you walk. Just until all this is over."

"I will."

"That's good," said Dad. "Better safe than sorry."

"I know."

Mom squeezed her hands together like she always did when she was nervous. "Be very careful while waiting for the school bus," she said. "And keep a close eye on your little sister, too. Don't worry, I watch your feet after you go to the other side of the bus."

"Why?"

"In case they grab you on that side."

Dad glanced at Mom. "The point is just to be careful."

I nodded. "We will."

There was a long pause.

"What did the FBI say?"

Dad looked at my mother. "Lots of stuff."

"Tell me what happened."

Mom and Dad didn't say much about the visit from the FBI at that time. We were still young, and they did all the could not to scare us but also to keep us safe and alert. But years later, they fleshed out the details of the visit.

And this is the story they told.

***

Our dogs barked and car doors slammed outside our home. Mom glanced out the window and saw a police car along with another vehicle. As the men walked towards our front door, my mother called for my father. Dad was taking a shower, and he couldn't hear her. Mom went to get him as the men walked down the sidewalk towards our front door.

As she knocked on the bathroom door, the doorbell rang.

"Harry!" she shouted. "Harry! The police are here!"

"What?" my father shouted over the running water.

"The police are at the door," she said. "Come out."

"The police are here?"

"Yes," she said. "It must be about John. Come out!"

The water shut off. "Okay, send them to the back door to give me time to dry off. I've got to get dressed. I'll be there as fast as I can."

"Okay," Mom said, and she hurried to the front door. Mom brushed her hair back with her fingers and opened the door. "Yes?"

"Mrs. Kerrigan, I'm Sherriff Roberts," said the man in the uniform. "These two men are with the FBI. May we please come in?"

"Yes," said Mom. "But could you please go around to the back door?"

The sheriff paused. "Of course."

"Thank you." Mom closed the door. *Oh great*, she thought, *that made me look suspicious*. As she hurried through the house towards the backdoor, she shouted, "Harry, come on!"

She opened the backdoor as the men climbed the stairs leading to the back porch. Besides the sheriff, both the other men were dressed in suits and ties.

"Come in," she said.

"Just to be clear," said Sheriff Roberts, "you are giving us permission to enter your home?"

"Sure," said Mom. "Please come in."

The men entered the house one by one. As they came to the threshold, each man said his name and asked for permission to enter. After they were all inside, Mom invited them to sit.

"Mrs. Kerrigan," said the man in a blue suit. He was clean-shaven and wore horn-rimmed glasses. "We're here to ask you a few questions about the Tymurs."

Mom wrinkled her face. "Tymurs?"

"Yes," said the man. "The Tylenol murders. The FBI calls it 'Tymurs.'"

"Oh, okay. How can I help you?"

"Do you know John Price?"

"Yes," said Mom. "We bought houses through him."

There was no response, so Mom added, "HUD houses."

There was still no response. "In Kansas City."

The agents looked at Mom but said nothing.

"And he managed them for us after we moved here."

"Mrs. Kerrigan," said the same agent. "We have been investigating Mr. Price and your name keeps coming up on his documents."

"Oh?"

"Yes."

"Well, as I said, we did business with them for years."

"And there are pictures."

"What pictures?"

"The Prices have pictures of you and your family. Of your husband." He paused and then added, "And they have pictures of your children."

"That's impossible," said Mom. "They never took pictures of us."

"Someone did," said the other agent. He had a dark mustache and was dressed in a black suit. "And somehow the Price's got the pictures."

"That's disturbing," said Mom.

"Is it?" said the agent in the blue suit.

"Yes, of course."

"Friends often have pictures of each other."

"We weren't friends," said Mom.

"You just said you were," said the agent in the blue suit.

"No, I didn't," said Mom. "I'm sorry, what was your name again?"

"Special Agent Jackson," said the man in the blue suit.

The mustached man added, "And I'm Special Agent Butler."

"Nice to meet you."

"Did they ever cheat you?" asked Butler. "You know, scam you out of money?"

"No," said Mom. "Not that I'm aware of."

Special Agent Butler shook his head. "That seems strange."

"Why's that?"

"Well," said Butler, "they cheated almost all their clients."

"Some even ended up dead," said Special Agent Jackson.

"That's right," said Butler. "At least one client was murdered."

"But Sarah said they dropped the charges against John in that case due to lack of evidence," said Mom.

Butler glanced at Jackson. "Oh, there was plenty of evidence."

"The police found evidence in the trunk of Price's car," said Jackson.

"Then why was John released?"

"They didn't read him his rights," said Jackson.

Butler glanced again at Jackson and then looked my mother in the eyes. "There were procedural problems with the case."

"Technicalities," said Jackson.

Butler maintained his gaze and didn't blink. "So, the judge had to dismiss the case."

Jackson cleared his throat. "But his other clients were lucky in a sense."

"How's that?"

"They weren't murdered," said Butler. "They were just cheated,"

"But not you," said Jackson.

"Right," said Butler. "But not you."

Mom waited a moment, and then she said, "I don't know what to tell you."

"May I be honest with you?" asked Agent Butler.

"Of course."

"I find a few things here very interesting." Agent Butler tapped a finger on his left hand for each point he made. "They didn't cheat you. They had pictures of you. Your names come up on so many documents. You are the only people they didn't hurt in one way or another."

Mom shrugged. "We bought houses from them. They managed them. It was just business."

At that moment, my father came into the room smelling of Old Spice aftershave. The FBI agents and the sheriff stood up.

"Mr. Kerrigan?" asked the sheriff.

"That's right."

"These men are from the FBI. They're here to ask you a few questions."

"What about?"

"About John Price."

"Oh," said my father, and rolled his eyes. "Man, that guy's a nut."

"A nut?"

"Yeah, you know. He's nuts. Not right in the head." Dad pointed his index finger at his head and made circles. "Crazy."

"That's right," said Mom. "He does crazy stuff."

"Like what?"

"Well, when he's driving, he can't turn left."

"That's weird," said the sheriff. "Not illegal, but strange."

"Yeah, and once when we were looking at a house, he jumped over the fence into a neighbor's yard," said Mom. "He picked a flower and jumped back. He then knelt on one knee and offered it to me like it was a rose and said, 'A flower for my fair lady.'

Dad rolled his eyes again. "He's strange."

"Yeah," said Mom. "And when I was talking on the phone in private with his wife, John suddenly started talking. He'd been listening in to our private conversation."

Jackson and Butler looked at each other.

"When did she call you?" asked Butler.

"Oh, lots of times."

"Recently?"

"No, not since the murders in Chicago. Not in a long time."

Jackson pushed his glasses up with his finger. "What did you talk about on your last call from her?"

"Well," said Mom. "She said she was having a 'girl's night out' in Springfield."

"And that didn't strike you as strange?" asked Butler.

"No, why would it?"

"Oh, come now," said Jackson. "Why would someone go from the big city to little hick town for a girl's night out?"

"I never thought of it that way."

"What did she want?"

"She wanted fifty-thousand dollars to start a business."

"What kind of business?"

"Something with an airplane," said Dad. "Her brother was involved."

"Her brother or a friend, or someone like that," added Mom.

"Did you have that kind of money to loan them?" asked Butler.

Mom shook her head. "No, but they thought we did."

"That was a weird phone call," said Special Agent Jackson.

Dad rubbed his head. "Well, he was a weird guy. I always knew there was something not quite right about him. But we had no reason not to trust him. It was just a feeling."

The agents looked at each other and nodded.

"Mr. and Mrs. Kerrigan, thank you for telling us all that," said Butler.

"No problem," said Dad.

"And you're right," said Jackson. "He has a mental illness of some kind." He paused and seemed to search his memory. He snapped his fingers. "Schizophrenia."

Dad nodded. "Well, we want to help you in any way we can. Do you have any other suspects?"

"Police investigated a man named Roger Arnold," said Butler. "He liked to go to bars, drink too much, and shoot his mouth off. One night, he was overheard making some suspicious remarks about the Tylenol murders."

"Yeah, he's another weird guy," said Jackson. "He was an amateur chemist and a right-winger. He worked in a warehouse with the parent of one of the victims. Kept illegal guns in his home. Stuff like that."

"Sounds like a promising lead," said Dad. "Maybe it was him."

Jackson scratched his head. "Yeah, but police were able to rule him out as a suspect."

"So, Price is the prime suspect," said Mom.

"Right."

"How sure are you he is the Tylenol murderer?" asked Dad.

"Well, he definitely wrote the extortion letter," said Jackson. "It was in his own handwriting. The fingerprints and the envelope he used both links back to Price, too. And he confesses in the letter to committing the murders."

"And threatening to do more," said Butler.

"Right," said Jackson. "At first, we thought he was just some weirdo. You know? A nut, as you would say."

"Yeah," said Dad.

Special Agent Butler nodded. "But then the Kansas City police told us about the Raymond West murder case. Then we took the letter more seriously. In fact, he was already on the run from the Kansas City police for other crimes when he wrote the letter."

"Price seems to have a grudge against his wife's former employer," said Jackson. "The letter may have been an attempt to frame him."

"Or maybe he was going to do to him what he allegedly did to Raymond West," said Butler. "Torture him into signing over the money." He glanced at his partner. "Automatic money laundering."

"How can we help you catch him?" said Dad.

Butler looked at them. "Has he ever been here?"

"Yes," said Mom. "He visited us not long before the Raymond West murder."

"Did you ever think that maybe he was planning to do to you what he did to Raymond West?"

"You mean, what he allegedly did to West," said Mom.

Jackson forced a smile. "Right. *Allegedly*."

"No," said Dad. "That never crossed our minds."

"Until now," said Mom. "Maybe when he saw our boys had grown big, he changed his mind."

Jackson nodded. "Criminals are a cowardly lot. They always take the path of least resistance. Your family is probably a lot tougher now than they remembered."

"Can you tell us anything about their visit?" asked Butler.

Dad rubbed his chin as he thought. "Not really," he said. "It was a short visit. But John did make one of his weird comments."

"Oh really? What did he say?"

"He talked about being able to hide out here in our woods."

The agents looked at each other again.

"We think he might try to do that," said Butler.

"Oh, no," said Mom. "I was afraid he would come here. What do you want us to do?"

"The best thing you could do to help us solve this case is to be on your guard, twenty-four seven."

"Right," said Butler. "Keep your security tight. Lock all the doors. Be prepared to defend yourselves by any means necessary."

"And most important of all, if he shows up here, don't call the local police." Jackson handed Mom a card with a phone number on it. "Call us."

"It would take the FBI hours to get here," said Mom.

"No, it won't," said Butler. "Call the number on the card, and FBI Agents will be here in thirty seconds. I promise."

Mom glanced at Dad. "Thirty seconds?"

Jackson nodded. "Guaranteed," he said. "We're setting up a base nearby."

"Well," said Special Agent Butler. "Thank you for talking with us."

"Goodbye," said Sheriff Roberts. "Thank you for your time. Don't worry. The FBI knows what they're doing."

"Thank you," said Dad.

"Very much," added Mom.

The three men walked to the door. The two agents nodded their heads to say goodbye as they left. As they stepped out the door, Agent Jackson looked back and smiled.

"Happy Halloween."

18
CAGE THE SPECTOR

The pleasant chill of fall became the whipping winds of winter, and John and Sarah were still on the run. On Monday, December 13th, 1982, I built a campfire. That afternoon, I had gone to boxing practice with some friends and felt relaxed from the physical workout. Darkness comes early in December, and the daylight was almost gone as I struck a match and lit the fire. I brought with me something to read, but it was too dark. It was Harold Kushner's book, *When Bad Things Happen to Good People*. It was published in 1981, the year before the Tylenol murders. I hadn't finished it yet, but I was most of the way through.

According to Rabbi Kushner, God is all-good but not all-powerful. Although God is with people in their suffering, God can't stop all evil and prevent all suffering single-handedly. But even though God can't do everything, God can do some very important things. For instance, God gives us strength to overcome our difficulties. God inspires others to help us in our time of need. And the way we deal with our suffering inspires others in their own lives. At fourteen years old, I was unsure if I agreed with everything in Rabbi Kushner's book, but I could understand the psychological and emotional value of his ideas. People could still find comfort and meaning in God's existence and loving presence, but without blaming God for causing or allowing their suffering. Overall, it was a helpful read to stimulate my own thinking about the problem of evil. I tucked it into the side pocket of my brown leather flight jacket.

Far away from the flickering light of my campfire, the police and the FBI searched frantically for John and Sarah. Despite hundreds of tips, nothing helped. The Prices seemed to have dropped off the face of the earth. But then, John returned to his pattern of behavior that had been so destructive to his life.

Blaise Pascal, the famous physicist, philosopher, and theologian, said, "All of humanity's problems stem from man's inability to sit quietly in a room alone." If John Price could have learned to "sit quietly in a room alone," things would have gone better for him in his life. But as he often did, John seemed to feel compelled to force himself into situations rather than waiting quietly for circumstances to resolve of their own accord.

While being wanted as prime suspects for the Chicago Tylenol Murders, Price goaded the police by writing letters to major newspapers. In his letters to the editors, he taunted the authorities about their reopening of the Raymond West murder case. He also proclaimed his innocence and stated that he and his wife were not armed." So, John and Sarah Price continued on in hiding, despite tipping his hand through his letters to the *Kansas City Star* and the *Chicago Tribune*. But their run from the law actually began much earlier, before the Chicago Tylenol Murders.

***

Although not much was known about their flight from justice at the time, years later I would learn more from an unlikely source. In the early twenty-first century, I was working for a mental health agency. My work included supervising therapists, conducting psychological assessments, and teaching psychology classes to professionals. One day, a college asked me to give a brief talk about the psychology of evil. After my talk, I recommended a book for further study.

The book I recommended was written by the psychiatrist M. Scott Peck. His book, *People of the Lie: Hope for Healing Human Evil*, explores evil from the perspective of psychology. Peck wrote the book in 1982, the year of the Chicago Tylenol Murders. It discusses clinical cases from Dr. Peck's clients in which he felt he encountered pure evil. He believed evil is real and needs to be faced head-on by psychology. According to Dr. Peck, Evil is not part of God's creation but is more like a cancer beyond God's control. Evil people attack others rather than face their own failures and insecurities.

After I had finished speaking, I asked for questions. When the question-and-answer segment was over, the students applauded and I prepared to leave. Dr. Shelly Thompson, the professor, thanked me and invited me to speak again in the future. As I gathered my things, Dr. Thompson introduced a student named Shannon Howard.

Shannon was a Criminal Justice major and minoring in Psychology. She was scheduled to give an oral report. Shannon had mid-length light brown hair and was dressed in a dark blue pantsuit. Under her suit jacket, she wore a light-blue, button-up shirt with the top two buttons undone, and a small gold cross hung around her neck. To my surprise, her topic was the Chicago Tylenol Murders.

After she announced her topic, a male student in the second row asked her, "Isn't that a myth?"

"A myth?" she asked.

"You know," he said. "An urban legend. It never really happened."

"It most certainly did really happen," said Shannon.

She then gave a basic overview of the crimes but said she wanted to focus on the prime suspects. Shannon was a strong, confident young woman. She spoke in an official and mature manner, far beyond her years. By her presentation style and tone, I could easily imagine her working in Law Enforcement.

"In December of 1981," she said, "police in Kansas City were investigating John Price and another man. The police had obtained a search warrant and used it to search Price's home. Price and the other man were suspected of credit card fraud involving one of John's clients. Authorities believed the two men were using that client's social security number and name illegally, and applying for credit cards."

"Yikes," said Dr. Thompson. "Identity theft scares me."

Shannon nodded. "Because of the search warrant and ongoing investigation, John and Sarah acted fast. They changed their names, skipped town, and fled to Chicago."

"Where the Tylenol murders happened," said Dr. Thompson.

"Correct," said Shannon. "There the two suspects used the aliases 'Robert and Nancy Richardson.' They lived in a cheap apartment and carried on under their new identities. In early 1982, a travel agency hired Sarah Price to do accounting work. Sarah's new boss, Frederick McCahey, was the heir to a major brewing company fortune. McCahey had bought the travel agency the prior year."

"She was able to work?" asked Dr. Thompson. "Didn't they check her background first?"

"Not back then, Ma'am. Times were different then."

That was before the change, I thought.

Shannon continued. "Despite using their new aliases to obtain work, times were hard on the Prices financially. In April, John finally found a temp job at a bank. But the hard times were just beginning. The travel agency Sarah worked for went bankrupt that same month."

"Bad luck," said a student in the front row.

Shannon nodded. "Before leaving work on her last day at the agency, Sarah took blank envelopes and stamped them with postage. She postmarked them with a date of April 15th, 1982. The next week, she cashed her final check. But her check bounced, and she was sued by the currency exchange agency where she had tried to cash the check."

"So, they were without a source of income," said Dr. Thompson. "They needed money. A common motive."

"That's right," said Shannon. "Anyway, Sarah, along with other former employees of the travel agency, filed claims in the hopes of collecting the money owed them. John Price undertook the task of being the advocate for the former employees. The hearing was held in August, but the outcome was not to the Prices benefit."

"August," said a student. "When did the Tylenol Murders happen?"

"September," said Shannon.

"That must have been a psychological stressor," said Dr. Thompson. "What happened at the hearing?"

"Since there were no funds to pay the claim, the bounced checks could not be rectified. After the hearing, an alleged argument arose between the Prices and McCahey."

Dr. Thompson shook her head. "They lost much-needed money. I bet that made them mad."

Shannon bobbed her head. "And that same month, John's temp job ended, leaving the Prices with no source of income at all. So, in early September 1982, John and Sarah changed their aliases to 'William and Karen Wagner.'"

"How many aliases did they have?" asked Dr. Thompson.

"Seventeen, I think," said Shannon. "They then bought two-way tickets under their new names to New York City. In New York, they switched their aliases back to 'Robert and Nancy Richardson.' John was unemployed during this time, but Sarah sought work. A real estate agency hired her."

"When was this?"

"I believe she began work for them on September 20th. Ten days later, on September 30th, the world learned something horrible was happening in Chicago."

"What was happening?" asked a student.

"Someone had laced Extra Strength Tylenol with cyanide poison," I said, "and murdered seven people."

"While fear gripped the nation," said Shannon, "John handwrote an extortion letter and mailed it to Johnson & Johnson. He used an envelope his wife had taken while working at the travel agency. The letter included some interesting specifics." Shannon thumbed through her notes and then read aloud. "For instance, it said, quote, 'So far, I have spent less than fifty dollars. And it takes me less than 10 minutes per bottle,' end quote. The letter went on to demand one million dollars to 'stop the killings.'"

"Very interesting," said Dr. Thompson. "Sounds like an open-and-shut case."

"But it's not so simple," I said.

"That's right," said Shannon. "The bank account number that John Price wanted the money sent to was not his own. It belonged to Sarah's former boss, Frederick McCahey."

Dr. Thompson clicked her tongue. "I bet he got a little visit from the police."

"Yes," said Shannon. "The authorities tracked the bank account and questioned McCahey. They swiftly ruled him out as a suspect, but they learned something that would prove important. When asked if he knew anyone who held a grudge against him, McCahey named Robert and Nancy Richardson."

"It's hard to keep all their aliases straight," said Dr. Thompson.

"It was a research nightmare," said Shannon, shaking her head. "Anyway, the authorities issued an arrest warrant for Robert Richardson and circulated a headshot of him. When the Kansas City police saw the headshot, they contacted the Chicago authorities. They told them the suspect's real name—John Price. They also told them of his run-ins with the law, and his arrest for the murder of a man named Raymond West."

"Who's that?" asked a girl sitting in the back of the class, dressed all in black.

Shannon looked to the back row. "He was a client of theirs who was murdered and dismembered after writing a check to Price for five-thousand dollars."

"Wow," said the student. "That's intense."

Shannon continued. "Police in Kansas City turned over Price's fingerprints, samples of his handwriting, and a box of evidence from the Raymond West case. At an FBI crime laboratory, they did fingerprint analysis." Shannon looked around the classroom. "I'd love to work there one day."

Dr. Thompson smiled at her. "I hope you get your chance."

Shannon smiled back. "Concerning the Raymond West murder case, something interesting turned up. On November 16th, a memo to the Kansas

City police from the FBI stated the following." Shannon pulled out a notecard and cleared her throat. "One latent fingerprint present on a lift on card #7, marked 'item 34 Pulleys and Rope in attic,' has been identified as an impression of the right thumb of John Price."

"Wow," I said.

Shannon glanced at me, and then went on. "Price's handwriting also allegedly matched that of another extortion letter. This one was sent to President Ronald Reagan. The precise contents of the letter were never made public, but reports claimed the letter made death threats against the president. It also demanded changes in the federal tax policy ..."

John was a taxman, I thought.

" ... warning that the Tylenol poisonings would continue if his demands were not met. The letter allegedly went on to threaten to attack the White House with remote-controlled airplanes."

"Why?" asked Dr. Thompson.

"In order to gridlock the radio transmissions used by the Secret Service."

"Man," said a male student with a scruffy goatee. "That guy was hardcore!"

Shannon glanced at him and before continuing. "Meanwhile, John and Sarah were on the run as prime suspects in the Chicago Tylenol Murders. The FBI was on a nation-wide manhunt for them. They also issued a warning that the Prices were considered to be armed and dangerous."

"It's weird no one saw them and contacted the police," said a student.

"They did," said Shannon. "In mid-October, a person from Sarah's job recognized her from television news coverage and contacted the police. They searched New York with an army of FBI agents and police officers. More than a hundred officers looked everywhere for them but found nothing. The Prices continued their pattern of changing their names and moving around. This time they called themselves 'Edward and Carol Scott.'"

A blond student with a ponytail in the back raised her hand.

"Yes?"

"I remember hearing that John Price wrote letters to newspapers while on the run."

"Right," said Shannon. "In my personal opinion, his letters have a mocking tone and taunt the authorities. The letter he wrote the week of Thanksgiving is especially interesting."

"Why's that?"

"Price signed his real name, which he didn't usually do. He also put his right thumbprint on it and sent copies to the Justice Department and the FBI."

The student with the goatee laughed. "Man, that's crazy!"

Dr. Thompson gave him a stern look. "Please continue, Shannon. We're running out of time, and this is fascinating."

"What happened next?" asked the blond with the ponytail.

"In November, surveillance cameras photographed the couple at a Western Union office. They were signing for a money order from Sarah's father."

"Where was this?"

"In Manhattan."

"So, police had concrete evidence that they were nearby."

"Yes," said Shannon. "And they also knew he loved reading newspapers."

"So?"

"So, his interest in the newspapers and his concern about what they wrote about him would be his undoing."

"I don't understand," she said.

Shannon smiled. "What happened next was very interesting. You see—"

"I'm sorry," said Dr. Thompson as she glanced at her watch, "but we are way over on time. Students for my next class are at the door. Thank you, Shannon."

The students applauded and stood. The rustling of books and papers filled the classroom and students began chatting with each other.

"Come on," said the girl dressed in black, sitting in the back row. "Let her finish."

"Sorry, everyone," said Dr. Thompson. "I'm afraid the conclusion to this story will have to wait."

***

Back in 1982, I sat in the dark watching the flames of my campfire. The logs were damp and crackled as they burned. As the sweet scent of hickory smoke wrapped around me like a warm blanket, I took a deep breath. The fire popped, sending a red-hot ember in front of my right boot. Stretching out my foot, I stepped on the glowing cinder. As I did, footsteps crunched on the dried leaves, twenty feet in front of me.

Sitting up straight, I strained to listen. In the distance, an owl hooted. Coyotes yipped in the valley. But the sound of footsteps continued, coming closer and closer to me. I searched around on the ground for my flashlight and touched it with my left hand. The footsteps were very close. I flicked on the flashlight and shone its beam towards the footsteps.

"Who's there?" I asked, scanning my flashlight right and left.

A man's voice answered. "It's me."

The flashlight shone on the brown shoes of a man. As I brought the light up, his legs and torso became visible. Not knowing who it was, I shined the light directly into his face. It was my father.

Dad squinted into the light. "They arrested John in New York City."

Lowering my flashlight, a wave of relief swept over me. "How'd they catch him?"

"A librarian recognized him and called the FBI. Police covered the exits and the FBI went to the fourth floor to search for him. He was sitting there with his back to them. An agent walked up and tapped him on the shoulder."

"What did he do?"

"John stood up and put on his glasses."

"No resistance?"

"No, none at all," said Dad. "He just stood there in silence as they cuffed him."

"So, it ends," I said, "not with a bang, but with a whimper."

"It's real life," said Dad. "It doesn't always end in a shootout like in the movies."

"Thank God for that."

We stood in silence for a moment, watching the crackling fire. The cold winter breeze tousled my hair, but I didn't mind.

"We can finally relax," I said, and I smiled at my father. "We can go back to normal."

"That's right," he said.

A shooting star sailed across the night sky, and then it was gone, as quick as it came. Dad looked at me and smiled. "It's over."

And if this story was a movie, it would be over. The plot would be tied up in a neat ribbon and bow with a clear-cut solution and a satisfying conclusion.

But this is real life and not a movie.

And the story isn't over yet.

PART III
THE 2000s
AFTER THE CHANGE

19
THE RIVER OF PAIN

Spring 2012

After John Price's arrest, the world changed forever. Johnson & Johnson's response to the Tylenol murders was lauded as an excellent example of how to respond to a crisis. It is still studied in college courses to this day. Although they lost millions of dollars, they came back stronger than ever. Their triple-sealed, over-the-counter medicine bottles revolutionized the industry. Tamper-resistant packaging became the norm for all similar products, saving untold numbers of lives every year. But despite these positive changes, the world had lost some of its innocence.

My personal world changed, too. In 1987, the same year John Price filed for a reduction in his prison sentence, I graduated from high school. I started freelance writing, selling short stories, articles, poetry, and scripts to magazines. In college, I studied psychology and then became a stage actor for many years. I married and raised a family.

Wanting to help others, I took a job in mental health. I worked as a supervisor of therapists and specialized in psychological assessments and education. Feeling called to ministry, I eventually went to seminary, worked as a hospital chaplain, and in 2010, I was ordained an Episcopal priest.

In the spring of 2012, I wanted to spend two days in prayer and meditation. I decided to go on a retreat at a monastery for the weekend. Paul Roberts, a friend from college, decided to come, too. During our college years, Paul and I read Jack Kerouac's book *On the Road*, and it inspired us to travel the country in his beat-up Ford pickup. In the years before I was married, he and I traveled all around America, camping in tents and having adventures. We went to New Orleans, the Rocky Mountains, Canada, and many other places. But over the years, we had lost touch, and this short retreat was a chance to reconnect. The first day was surprisingly busy, and we didn't have a chance to talk.

On our second and final day there, the bells of the monastery rang, radiating through the cool spring air. The bells signaled the end of noonday prayer and the start of lunch. The midday meal was vegetable soup, bread, and water. As we ate, we caught each other up on our personal lives. We each spoke about our wives, families, and work.

Paul always dressed business casual. He wore a light-blue polo shirt, tan slacks, and brown loafers.

The same long hair style he had in college framed his aging face. He brushed a strand of brown hair, flecked with grey, back from his forehead and glanced up from his soup at me. "Oh, I saw a program you'd be interested in."

Dipping my bread into my steaming hot soup, I looked at Paul. "What's it about?"

"John Price and the Tylenol murders. It talked about what happened back in 2009."

"Oh yes, I remember that." I put my bread down. "The FBI reactivated the case and raided his home."

Paul nodded his head. "Man, it's a fascinating case. I did some research and got into it. I read books, articles, watched some shows, stuff like that. There's a lot out there about it. Did you know they charged him in 2004 for attacking a woman?" Paul was an engineer and interested in the fine details of everything.

"No, what happened?"

"He was accused of drugging and kidnapping her. Allegedly, he told the woman he was going to wrap her in a plastic bag, and take her out to the forest and let the animals eat her."

"My Lord," I said, and made the sign of the cross. "That's horrible."

My mind flashed to the woman I found in the hole when I was five. She was wrapped in a plastic bag, too. Plastic bags were also part of the Raymond West murder case. And plastic bags were found in the trunk of Price's car, along with rope, and checkbooks belonging to West.

Paul continued, drawing me out of my thoughts. "He spent three years in jail awaiting trial, but the prosecutors dismissed the case on the day of his trial. Apparently, the victim was afraid to testify."

I shook my head. "What else did you learn?"

"Well, I knew little about his arrest and trial for extortion, so I read about that. Sarah Price surrendered the day after John was arrested. She wouldn't answer questions, and they charged her with illegally using a client's social security number to create an alias."

John asked my parents for their social security numbers, I thought. *I'm so glad they didn't steal their identities.*

"Illegal and unethical," I said, "but just a misdemeanor."

"Yeah," he said. "But they got Al Capone on taxes. The Devil's in the details."

Paul finished his soup and sipped his cup of water. "Did you know prosecutors wanted her bond set at five million dollars?"

"Wow, that's a lot of money, especially back then," I said. After eating a spoonful of soup, I looked at Paul. "It's an interesting case, for sure. But investigators couldn't prove John Price was in Chicago at the time of the murders."

"Right," he said. "But there's also a lot that seems to point to him as the killer."

"I know," I said, "but the airlines showed no tickets for anyone matching any of John Price's known aliases. Also, witnesses say they saw him in New York around the time of the murders."

"Well, witnesses reported seeing them all over the country. Those reports were all wrong. So, even though he was caught in New York, it's hard to believe the New York sightings were all accurate." Paul shook his head. "But without a commercial airplane, I can't imagine how he could have got there and back so quickly. Can you?"

"My opinion doesn't matter."

"Come on," said Paul. "If you had to guess."

"Are you asking me to speculate?"

"Sure, speculate."

I remembered the phone call Sarah made to my mother, years before. She and John wanted fifty-thousand dollars to buy a private airplane. Mom said Sarah told her they knew someone who could fly it for them. "Do you think he could have used a private airplane?"

"Interesting," said Paul. "That would explain why there were no tickets listed under any of his aliases."

"But it would take a certain amount of money to hire a private airplane," I said. "Unless they knew someone who was a private pilot, that is."

"I hadn't thought of that," said Paul. "A private pilot and personal airplane. A favor from a friend."

"And besides, whoever the killer was, he probably would've placed the tainted boxes in the back of the row."

Paul paused and thought for a moment. "So, in that case, it would've taken a few days for the poisoned bottles to be the ones bought."

"Probably," I said. We finished our bread and water. "Okay, enough speculation. They charged John Price with extortion for the murders, but not the actual Tylenol murders."

"Yeah," he said. "At his arraignment, Price pleaded not guilty. His defense attorney argued Price wrote the extortion letter to get his wife's former boss in trouble. Of course, he also said his client didn't commit the Tylenol murders or even expect to make any money from his extortion letter."

Smiling, I took a sip of water. "Interesting."

Paul rolled his eyes. "I know," he said. "If that was true, why did he go on the run? He could've just told the authorities it was a prank. He would've just got a slap on the wrist and been done with it. But instead, he fled the law and wrote taunting letters to newspapers."

I nodded. "So, John Price was found guilty of extortion and sentenced to prison."

"Yes," he said. "While awaiting sentencing, he worked in the bakery at the prison. But his fellow inmates wouldn't eat his baked goods."

"I can just hear the jokes now. 'Hey Mack, these pastries are to die for!'"

Paul laughed. "I know, right?"

"I remember hearing that while he was in jail, John volunteered to help the authorities solve the Tylenol murders."

"That's right," he said. "So weird. He would discuss the case with them for hours, speculating on how the killer committed the crimes. Price even drew a diagram showing exactly how cyanide could have been placed in capsules from the comfort of the killer's car. He said the whole process could be done in just a few minutes in a drugstore parking lot, and the tainted capsules would be returned to store shelves. No one would be the wiser."

I remembered hearing about the pharmaceutical business John and his partner had started years before. "Spooky," I said.

"That's what the authorities thought," said Paul. "They wanted him to take a lie detector test, but he wouldn't."

"Maybe it would've helped his case to take the polygraph test."

Paul let out his good-natured laugh. "Ah, that's what I love about you. Always looking for the best in everyone."

"Thanks." I smiled, and then added, "I think."

"He got a total of twenty years, right? For that and for mail and tax fraud?"

"Yeah," I said. "And it wasn't easy on him. They say the prisoners would goad him, calling him 'Tylenol man.'"

"When did he get out of prison?"

"In October of 1995." I looked Paul in the eye. "On Friday the 13th."

"Fascinating," said Paul.

I nodded. "He served thirteen years of a twenty-year sentence."

"Was Price the only suspect?"

"Initially, there were lots of suspects.

"But the authorities weeded the list down to Price."

I finished my cup of water. "Another guy, Roger Arnold, was identified and investigated. After investigators checked him out, he was cleared of the Tylenol murders. He had a mental breakdown and killed the person he thought turned him in to the police. But it was a case of mistaken identity, and Arnold went to prison for second-degree murder."

"That reminds me, there was a woman named Laurie Dann who was investigated, too."

"That's right," I said. "In 1988, she shot and poisoned several people, but police discovered it was unrelated to the Tylenol murders."

"And in 2011, they investigated and ruled out the Unabomber, too."

"Yes."

"So, that brings us back to John Price. Did you know he wrote a novel about people being poisoned? He even mentions the Chicago Tylenol Murders in the book!"

"I know." I shook my head. "He must crave attention. But he doesn't seem to care if it's good or bad."

Paul was quiet for a moment. He then looked at me with his kind eyes. "Jack, you told me that John Price visited you when you were five. After you found the body."

"Yes," I said. I shook my head. "Based on his history, his kindness that day surprised me. I always thought that was nice of him to visit me when I was sick." I paused and looked at Paul. "He gave me a flashlight."

Paul nodded. "He looked at you without blinking. He kept smacking the flashlight into his left hand."

"Right."

Paul spoke slowly, in a gentle, compassionate tone. "John wasn't being nice to you." He reached out and put his hand on my arm. "He was threatening you."

The image of John Price kneeling by my bed, staring at me with his intense eyes, flooded my mind. He was looking at me without blinking, smacking the handle of his massive flashlight into his left hand. *Smack, smack, smack.*

In a flash of insight, I realized the source of my anxiety. It sprang from something that happened in my childhood. I always remembered the facts, but I repressed the feelings. Throughout my life, the emotions came back to haunt me. When I was five years old, my mind put the feelings away to deal with later. And so, they came out unexpectedly when something would trigger them.

Anxiety was an emotional echo, an actual memory of the repressed feelings of a five-year-old child going through a terrifying situation—a deep remembrance of something scary that happened in the distant past.

A feeling of liberation and emotional freedom wrapped around me like a warm blanket on a winter's day. *Anxiety isn't a wound*, I thought. *It's a gift*. Having it wasn't my fault, but it was to my benefit. It made me a better person. It wasn't collateral damage; it was a boon.

And with this insight, the waves of anxiety reached a crescendo and then crashed. I realized the good news. The feelings I repressed as a child were a normal response that any emotionally healthy person would have to such a threatening situation. *I've always been okay*, I thought, *I just haven't always known it*. I wasn't broken; I was blessed.

I took comfort in knowing that the dangerous situation I went through as a child was all over. I had survived. Everything was okay. I didn't need to feel frightened, anxious, or guilty. I finally understood that I did everything a five-year-old child could possibly do to help the poor woman I found in the shallow grave.

I had found the headwaters of the river of pain.

The guilt, anxiety, and anger washed away from me. *When I was five years old,* I thought, *I gazed into the eyes of a suspected killer, and I didn't even blink.* And if I could do that at five, I could do anything now. The fear vanished, and I felt empowered, courageous, unstoppable. No longer would my memories be a source of pain, but a spark to ignite the flames of enlightenment.

My early experiences started me on a lifelong quest that led to personal growth, emotional maturity, and spiritual transformation. I touched levels of consciousness that I couldn't have reached otherwise. The events of my life made me a better person. Gratitude for the wisdom I received from them filled my heart. I was at peace with God, myself, and the entire world. Words from Genesis filled my mind—*What you have meant for evil, God has used for good.*

I nodded my head. "I know."

20
THE POWERS THAT BE

Our delicious monastic lunch was over and we went outside for a walk. We stood and took our bowls, plates, and cups to the monastery kitchen. After thanking the monks for their hospitality, we went outside into the crisp spring air.

"So, do you think John Price did it?" said Paul.

"I don't know who did it. No one does."

We entered a small grove of trees near the monastery motherhouse. A short trail covered with snow-white gravel led through the forest, taking the faithful past the *Stations of the Cross*. Also known as the *Way of the Cross*, the Stations are a spiritual journey using a sequence of images showing Christ on the day of his crucifixion.

We came to the first stop. "First Station," I said. "Jesus is condemned to death."

Paul glanced at the wooden plaque showing the first image. "Well, in 1989, examiners for the U.S. Parole Commission apparently believed he was the Tylenol murderer. They recommended he serve his maximum sentence because of the preponderance of the evidence."

"I heard that."

We walked on, the white gravel crackling beneath our feet. "Second Station," I said. "Jesus takes up his Cross."

Paul stopped and tied the lace on his shoe. When he finished, he looked up at me. "When I was researching the case, I saw a clip from WCVB Channel 5 of Boston. They reported that in early 2009, some court documents were released."

"Oh, yeah?"

"Yeah, and apparently the documents showed that Department of Justice investigators concluded he was responsible for the poisonings. They seemed to think he did it, even though they didn't have enough evidence to officially charge him with the murders."

Bird songs filled the air. "I've always admired your memory."

We came to the next stop. "Third Station," I said. "Jesus falls for the first time."

Paul looked at me and smiled. "And I read the FBI hired a psychiatrist to consult on the case. He wrote that in his opinion, Price was capable of committing the Tylenol killings."

We stopped and looked out through a clearing in the forest at a field of spring flowers. Butterflies danced from flower to flower.

"That's all very interesting," I said. "But the mystery I'm trying to solve is not whether John Price committed the Tylenol murders."

Paul looked at me. "The mystery you're trying to solve is the mystery of evil. 'If God is all-good and all-powerful, why do bad things happen to good people?'"

"Right."

"I've always wondered about that, too," said Paul.

"A lot of ink has been spilled trying to answer that question. Some say God gives us evil and suffering as a punishment for our sins, but I don't believe that."

"Me neither."

"I mean, a lot of good people suffer and a lot of evil people get away scot-free." I shook my head. "There are often negative consequences to our behavior, but that's different from God smiting us with a health condition or physical harm when we do something wrong."

"Thank goodness."

We walked on, looking at the next three stations as we passed.

"Others say suffering is a byproduct of free will," I said. "And there's certainly some truth to that. People can and do abuse the gift of free will, and evil is often the result."

Paul furrowed his brow. "Yeah, but what about 'Acts of God,' like hurricanes?"

"Natural disasters aren't 'Acts of God,' no matter what insurance companies may say.'" I smiled. "Acts of God are when people pull together to help each other afterward."

Looking at the next image, I read the plaque aloud. "Seventh Station: Jesus falls for the second time."

As Paul looked at the seventh image, he spoke. "Some say God gives us suffering to make us better people."

A hawk called from high above us, as it soared through the blue sky.

"God can and does bring good out of evil," I said, "but God doesn't send evil to teach us a lesson."

The gravel crunched as we walked on.

"Growing up," said Paul, "I was taught that God is in complete control of everything that happens. God has a plan that includes God causing or allowing evil and suffering."

A fallen branch lay on the ground in front of us. I picked it up and set it aside. "God doesn't plan or permit our suffering," I said, "but God does want to heal it. Think of God as being like a doctor or nurse. They don't cause our suffering, but they are working to heal it."

We continued over the gravel path until we came to the next stop on our pilgrimage. "Eighth Station," I said. "Jesus meets the women of Jerusalem."

"I like the idea of God not causing suffering," said Paul, "but ingrained beliefs die hard."

"I know," I said. "And those ideas you mentioned are the belief of many people today. But they didn't come about until the 4th century."

Taking a few steps forward, I glanced back and noticed Paul still standing at the last station. I turned to face him.

"Really?" he said. "I assumed the Church always taught that."

"A lot of people think that. Some people today act like God is the genie from Aladdin's Lamp. They expect God to grant them their wishes at a snap of divine fingers—" I snapped my fingers and then proclaimed in a loud voice, "'Your wish is my command!'"

Paul laughed and started walking again. "When something terrible happens, we hear things, like, 'I know this is God's will.'"

"Right," I said. "People say things like, 'God needed another angel in his choir.'"

"'God did this to teach me a lesson.'"

"Yeah, stuff like that. It lays evil on God's shoulders alone. Which may sound nice at first."

"It's comforting," said Paul. "At least, until you apply it to specific cases of unspeakable evil that happen in real life. Then it becomes scary."

"Like the Tylenol murders."

"Yes," he said. "Or the murder victim you found when you were a child."

"Right," I said. "But then, when you think about it, you realize some things. If God is all-controlling, then God either caused, or at very least permitted, all evil, sin, and suffering."

Paul ran his fingers through his brown hair. "That would mean every murder, torture, war, sin, and all acts of violence have all been caused or allowed by God."

"Right," I said. "It means God knows about every atrocity, and has the power to stop them, but doesn't." A bird chirped on a branch above us. "But if you asked someone living at the time of Christ, their view would be very different."

"What did they believe?"

I laughed. "Do you really want a history lesson?"

"We're in a monastery," said Paul, and smiled. "When in Rome ..."

We walked to the next station. Paul read the plaque aloud: "Jesus falls for the third time."

"The ancient Jews and early Christians believed evil is not a part of God's plan, but a departure from it. God wills the best for us and our world." I stopped and looked at Paul. "But there are other 'wills' in our world besides God's."

"What do you mean?"

"Well, they believed that in the beginning, God created a vast number of powerful spiritual beings. The Old Testament calls them the *elohim*, which means 'the gods.' Or sometimes they're called the 'Divine Council' or the 'Sons of God.' And the New

Testament calls them 'The Principalities and Powers.' Today, we usually call them the 'fallen angels.'"

"The Powers that Be."

"Yes," I said.

"Sort of an early biblical polytheism?"

"No," I said. "They believed in one supreme, eternal Creator God who, in a sense, wanted a family. So, God created a vast number of spiritual 'children,' powerful beyond our comprehension."

"The 'Sons of God.'"

"Right," I said. "Anyway, God put this highest order of powerful angels, the 'Sons of God,' in charge of running the entire world. You might say, in charge of 'running the family business.'"

"But some of these powerful angels rebelled."

"Yes," I said. "And ancient people saw suffering and evil in the world as a result of this rebellion. They believed there is a vast cosmic war going on between the Creator God and the fallen angels. Sort of a spiritual 'civil war.'" I quoted the Book of Revelation. *"Now war arose in heaven."*

Paul nodded. "It reminds me of the psalm we read today during morning prayer."

"Psalm 82."

"Yeah," said Paul. "'*God has taken his place in the divine council; in the midst of the gods he holds judgment.*' I always wondered who those 'gods' were."

"To the ancients, they were powerful, highly intelligent, immortal spiritual beings who are locked in combat against God and the good angels."

We came to the Tenth Station. I read the plaque aloud: "Jesus is stripped of his garments."

Paul looked at me and smiled. "And I always thought angels were nice."

"Some are!" I said, smiling back. "But to understand the ancient worldview, you need to forget any thought of angels as cute babies with wings. To them, angels are fierce. They're not sweet, they're not cute, and they're not imaginary."

Paul shook his head. "I don't understand why God would create such powerful evil beings."

"Well, they were originally created good. God gave them power and authority over everything from nations to health to hurricanes. God did this with the best intentions. We read about this in Deuteronomy. But later, many of these created 'Sons of God' fell and rebelled against their Creator."

"They were created good and they've fallen,'" said Paul, "so they need to be destroyed."

"No," I said, shaking my head. I looked at Paul. "They need to be redeemed."

There was a long pause. "Whoa."

I nodded my head. "They wanted the humans to worship them instead of their Creator," I said. "They wanted to maintain full control—their 'legal' authority— over their allotted portion of the world. And they were willing to fight to do so."

It was time for me to drive back home. We stopped at the Eleventh Station: *Jesus is nailed to the Cross.* I pointed at the image. "And that's how God broke the authority of the fallen angels. When they crucified Christ, they overstepped the jurisdiction God had given them over humanity. Hidden under the bait of Christ's humanity was the hook of his divinity, and it snared the leaders of the fallen angels. The decisive battle was won on the cross—you might say, D-Day—but struggles with the lesser Powers rage on."

After a moment of silence, we continued.

"But God knows everything, right?" asked Paul as we passed the Twelfth Station. "Didn't God know ahead of time that these powerful spiritual beings would rebel?"

"That's another common idea," I said, "but it's not a universal belief. Some think God is moving through time with us, into an open and undetermined future. You might say, 'God knows everything that can be known.'"

We read the Thirteenth Station as we passed: *Jesus is taken down from the Cross.*

"That would mean God knew rebellion was possible," said Paul, "but since it hadn't happened yet, it would be impossible to know for sure."

"That's the idea," I said. "And many of these lesser fallen angels are still in rebellion against the Creator, and at war with humanity and with each other. At least, that's what the ancients thought. They believed our world is caught in the crossfire."

"Like 'No Man's Land' in World War I."

I nodded. "Knowing this, it did not surprise the early Christians when evil happened. They expected it, and they found meaning in their suffering because they knew about the angelic war. So, they didn't try to explain evil away, but to wrestle against it."

Paul quoted the New Testament: *"For we do not wrestle against flesh and blood, but against the rulers, against the authorities, against the cosmic powers over this present darkness, against the spiritual forces of evil in the heavenly places."*

"Ephesians," I said.

Paul nodded. "So, God didn't orchestrate evil for an unknown reason."

We passed the Fourteenth Station: *Jesus is laid in the tomb.*

"Right," I said. "To the early Christians, evil and suffering were not caused by God for some mysterious higher purpose."

"They're the result of free beings choosing contrary to the will of God."

I nodded. "And some of those free beings are not human."

We were silent for a few moments as we made our way through a grove of pine trees. At the exit of the little trail, the monks had added a fifteenth station to the traditional fourteen. We paused and read in silence the final plaque—*The Resurrection of Jesus*.

"Fascinating," said Paul. "I wonder if they were right about all that."

He and I walked toward the parking lot. "I think the point here is that there are larger forces at work. Evil's not just personal. It's also social, cultural, and institutional."

"Right," said Paul. "Institutionalized evil."

"Exactly."

"So, do you think you found the answer?"

"I don't have all the answers, but I do have faith." I looked at Paul. "Rather than relying on any single system to fully explain the mystery of evil, I think it's better to find the best parts of all the best answers and integrate them into one. Taken together as a whole, we can start to find a meaningful solution to the problem of evil."

Paul shook his head. "Yeah, but there's one thing I'll never understand. God could just reach out and stop evil, but won't. I just don't get that."

"God's working by different rules," I said. "God is love. Love never forces the loved one. You don't force your girlfriend to marry you; you ask her and you honor her free response." Paul looked confused, so I paraphrased. "True love involves giving the loved one the freedom to choose. But because of this freedom, some angels and humans have freely chosen to act contrary to the will of God."

"According to the ancients."

"Right," I said. "So, God needs our free cooperation to help stop suffering and evil."

Paul mused. "We're God's hands in the world."

I nodded. "And God is always working alongside us—inspiring, guiding, and supporting us. But even though we are called to cooperate with God in this way, we are *never* equal to God. That was the mistake of the fallen angels."

"Yes," said Paul. "It reminds me of something in the New Testament, 'Do not be overcome by evil, but overcome evil with good.'"

"Perfect."

He looked at me and smiled. "You seem at peace."

"I am," I said, as we walked into the monastery parking lot. "To me, the question is no longer, 'Why does God allow suffering?' The question for me now is, 'What can we as people of faith do to help those who are suffering?'"

Paul and I said goodbye, and we promised we wouldn't wait so long before reconnecting again. As I drove down the dirt road leaving the monastery, I thought about our conversation and my weekend of prayer and meditation. My gas tank was full, so when I reached the highway, I started the long drive home without stopping on the way.

***

As I drove, my shoulders felt tense and my head began to ache. By the time I reached my house, I had a bad headache and was glad to be home. My wife, Eve, greeted me and asked about my weekend. We discussed my stay at the monastery. She noticed I was rubbing my temples.

"Do you have a headache?"

"Yeah," I said. "Do we have any painkillers?"

"I just bought a fresh bottle today."

She handed me the small cardboard box, and I opened it as we talked.

"Thank you," I said. "What did you do while I was at the monastery?"

Eve shrugged. "I've just been chatting with someone I met online." She furrowed her brow. "So, what did you learn in the monastery?"

"I did some inner work that was helpful. I learned something about myself."

"Oh, yeah? What did you learn?"

Removing the bottle of painkillers from the box, I tossed the empty packaging into the recycle bin.

"When I was five years old and found the murdered woman, you might say that I ate from the tree of the knowledge of good and evil. What I mean is, I learned at that young age that evil is real, and the world is not all sunshine and rainbows."

The safety seal was stubborn, and I couldn't remove it with my fingers. Reaching into my pocket, I pulled out my pocketknife to help with the task.

"I can't go back to the innocence of childhood. I can't go back to the 'Garden of Eden.' It's guarded by an angel with a flaming sword, whose name is 'Time.' But I realized something very important."

I flicked my knife open and searched the medicine bottle to find the best point to remove the plastic safety seal. There was a perforated line running down the side, and I tried to loosen it.

"Although I can't go back, I can go forward." I looked at my wife and smiled. "And that's what God's calling me to do."

Slipping the blade under the plastic seal, I turned my knife to snap it off. It split and I picked at the broken seal with my fingers, pulling it loose from the cap. Rotating it to the proper location, I clicked the bottle open. Underneath was another safety seal. After picking off the inner seal with my fingers, I removed the cotton and poured two painkillers into my left hand. Noticing Eve watching me, I dropped the painkillers back into the bottle. I smiled at her.

"I think I'll just have a glass of water."

21
THE TERRIFYING LOVE OF GOD

Present Day

Over the past several years, I continued my work as a priest. My ministry gave me many opportunities to revisit the problem of evil and suffering. I felt like I almost had a satisfying answer, but there was still a piece of the puzzle missing. I decided to contact my friend Tom and ask him to meet with me. Despite his background as a serious scholar, Tom has a gift for explaining complex ideas in a simple way that anyone can understand. He made time to meet with me in the great outdoors. I packed a knapsack and headed out to meet him.

The early morning sunshine lit the mountain pass and bird songs filled the air. Shifting my brown leather knapsack to my right shoulder, I continued hiking the trail that led up the side of the rocky crag. Near the top of the mountain ridge, there was a clearing where I was to meet Tom.

Tom—Dr. Thomas Jay Oord—is a seminary professor, philosopher, and best-selling author, having written or edited over twenty-five books. One of his specialties as a theologian is the problem of evil. His provocative books have offered a challenging new way of understanding questions about God, evil, and suffering.

As I crested the mountain ridge into the clearing, Tom was already there. Dressed in a light blue shirt, green cargo pants, and brown hiking boots, Tom looked as comfortable in the great outdoors as he was in a college classroom. He had his camera set up, and he was engaging in one of his favorite avocations—nature photography. Near the base of his tripod, his hiking staff rested on his orange backpack.

"Hi Tom," I called as I walked closer.

Tom looked up and a warm smile spread across his bearded face. "Hello!"

Taking off my hat, I let the breeze cool my head from my hike up the mountain. "Thanks for making time to meet with me."

He shook my hand. "My pleasure."

Tom's camera and tripod caught my eye. "How'd you get interested in nature photography?"

He bent down and looked through the camera lens. "Well, it goes back to my high school days. I worked for the school newspaper and yearbook. I realized the camera could be my tool to explore my artistic side."

"Very cool."

He looked up from his camera and smiled. "So, what's up?"

"I've mentioned to you before about me finding a murdered woman when I was five. From there, my story expands into the Tylenol murders back in 1982."

"Yes," said Tom. He shook his head. "Finding a murder victim at five is a lot for a child to process."

I nodded. "And many people have been through a lot worse. Including the victims and their families."

Tom looked serious. "That's all too true."

"Anyway, it started me at that young age on a spiritual search to understand the mystery of evil." I looked out over the horizon.

"That's a big question for a child," said Tom. "It's a big question for anyone."

"Finding a way to reconcile the God of my understanding with the existence of suffering and evil has been a lifelong quest." I glanced back at Tom. "I've been searching for answers my entire life. But it hasn't been easy."

Tom nodded. "I can relate. As a young person, I took my faith seriously, too. But in college, I turn to atheism. The reasons I had to believe in God no longer made sense."

I smiled. "But you're a theologian now. What brought you back?"

"I returned to faith in my search for meaning and my quest to make sense of love. Since my return to belief, I've been trying to develop a more coherent explanation for life."

"I'm on that same spiritual journey," I said. "Finding the murdered woman when I was five was just the beginning. Trying to make sense of it all has been a driving force in my life. I've studied psychology, philosophy, and spirituality, seeking meaningful answers. That's where you come in. This area is your specialty. What can you tell me about the problem of evil?"

"Well," said Tom. "In a nutshell, it asks this question: Why doesn't a perfectly loving and perfectly powerful God prevent the genuine evil in our lives and in the world?"

"Yes," I said. "That's been my question, too. I've explored the usual answers, but I've found some of them unsatisfying."

Tom nodded his head. "The usual answers to that question don't satisfy me, either."

"What are some of the answers that you've explored and rejected?"

"Oh, lots of them." Tom looked through his camera lens. "Some think that only bad people suffer. But that clearly isn't true. Others think that all suffering is a part of some mysterious plan. They think it all works out good in the end."

"Right," I said. "I've heard many people say that."

"Yeah, me too," said Tom. "But I doubt that. And I can see how evil makes the world worse. Others say God allows pain and suffering to teach us a lesson or build our characters."

I remember my conversation with my priest when I was fourteen. That was his view. "What do you think about that?"

"I think there's some truth to that idea. But so many people who suffer don't get better, aren't wiser, or don't see their lives improve."

A hawk flew overhead, making a shrill call. I glanced up at the hawk, watched it fly for a moment, and then I continued. "When someone is a victim of real evil, what can they do to work together with God for their healing?"

"Many people who endure pointless pain or are the victims of violence seek therapy," said Tom. "And I encourage that. But often the big question about God's work isn't addressed in therapy. So, I think a new way of thinking about God should supplement the kind of therapy we need."

I nodded my head. "I agree. My question has never been, 'Who committed the Tylenol murders?' My question has always been, 'Why would anyone?'"

"Yes," said Tom. "Right."

"It's the big question that has been driving my search for understanding."

Tom smiled. "That's true for many I've met. They want a real answer to the big question so many people ask. They wonder why a loving and powerful God—if that God exists—didn't stop the unnecessary suffering they and others have endured."

"Exactly. What do you tell them?"

"I think a meaningful answer to this question can be found in a few related ideas."

"Like what?"

"Well, the first idea says that God simply *can't* single-handedly prevent evil."

"That's different than most pop theology out there," I said. "It tends to say 'God won't' stop evil and suffering instead of 'God can't'."

"Right," said Tom.

"But why can't God?"

"God always loves everyone and everything, but God's love is uncontrolling. So, God can't control anyone or anything."

"I see what you're saying," I said. "But I feel God has been very active in my life."

"Mine too," said Tom. "It isn't that the God I believe in is uninvolved. I'm not saying God is in a spaceship flying around the planet, looking at things from a distance."

Smiling, I nodded my head. "God is not an ancient astronaut from the History Channel."

Tom laughed. "Yeah, right. I think God is present to everyone and everything in every moment. But God's active presence is always uncontrolling love."

"So, uncontrolling love is at the center of your answer to the problem of evil."

"Yes," said Tom.

I wanted to paraphrase Tom to be sure I understood. "God's nature is not just love in a generic sense, but *uncontrolling* love. And God loves everyone and everything."

"Right," he said, "and so, God can't control anyone or anything."

"That means God is uncontrolling, but always with us. God is always inspiring us, empowering us, and working alongside us for the healing of ourselves and our world. God is our fellow sufferer who understands."

"Yes," said Tom. "And that also means God isn't to blame for the evil in the world. God didn't cause it, and God can't prevent it single-handedly."

"We need to cooperate with God to deal with evil and suffering in the world."

"Exactly," said Tom. "God suffers with us when we suffer. God really feels our pain. And God tries to heal to the extent possible."

"God is the most loving, the most active, and the most powerful being in existence," I said. "God can and does act in powerful ways."

"I agree," said Tom. "But God can't stop evil single-handedly."

"So, we need to partner with God to stop evil."

"Right," said Tom. "And God also can't heal single-handedly. So, the conditions of creation must be right for healing, or there must be cooperation from our bodies, our minds, or the natural world."

"But sometimes good does come from bad. God does seem to work with us in this way."

"Yes," said Tom. "I agree. God works with any situation to try to squeeze good out of the bad God didn't want in the first place. It means God never gives up when things are going wrong. But God works with us to bring something good from the evil we sometimes suffer."

My mind returned to the unsolved murders. *Like the product tampering reforms that came into place directly because of the Chicago Tylenol Murders. Or the kindness of people who reached out to comfort the victims' families during their time of need. Or how exploring these questions has helped me grow morally, intellectually, and spiritually.*

Tom continued, pulling me out of my thoughts. "I think God really needs our cooperation for love to win. Our choices and decisions matter to the outcome of our lives and to history. God calls upon us to collaborate for the good of all."

I thought of the case again. *Hundreds of agents working together to solve the murders. The nurse and the firefighters who first suggested that the cause of death for the seven victims was Extra Strength Tylenol laced with cyanide. People like my parents cooperating with the FBI in whatever way they could. All these were working together to do God's will in the world.*

"But even so," I said. "Sometimes the conditions aren't right." I paused, thinking of the unsolved murders. "At least, not yet."

"That's right," said Tom. "But I and many others who think about God as one who works through uncontrolling love no longer blame God when we suffer. We hurt. We suffered trauma."

"And it's human nature to look for someone to blame."

Tom nodded. "But we don't need to blame God. Because a God of uncontrolling love isn't the source of evil. In fact, that God can't stop evil all alone."

"God needs our help."

"Yes," said Tom. "I have some friends who pretend like the world is all roses and warm fuzzies. They think the pain and suffering we endure aren't really real." Tom shook his head. "I think they live in fantasyland. We need real answers to our biggest questions, not pie-in-the-sky illusions."

Tom adjusted his photography equipment. "Some people think they solve the problem of evil by giving reasons for why evildoers might do their evil. And I do think we need to look at the motives involved. That's part of working with God to try to overcome evil and be instruments of healing."

"It's important work," I said. "A piece of the puzzle, but it's not enough in itself."

"Yes," said Tom. "We also need good explanations for why God doesn't stop evil." Tom paused and looked at me. "I don't know about you, but I sometimes hear people say, 'God didn't cause this evil. But God *allowed* it.'"

I nodded my head. "I know. I've heard that many times, too."

"I don't find this comforting. We all know that loving people prevent the evils that they can prevent. Of course, there are lots of things we can't stop. But if we have the power and agency to prevent horrific evils and yet allow them, we aren't consistently loving."

"How do people react to your ideas about evil and suffering?"

"To be honest, some of the ideas I'm offering can be unsettling. The God I am portraying is not in control. And many people want the security and safety that comes from thinking God is in control."

"But how about people who have been victims of evil and violence?"

"To most survivors, victims, and others who have been harmed, these ideas are good news. They give hope. They make sense. They point to a God of love who is not responsible for the evil in our lives."

"That in itself gives people comfort and hope," I said. "For many survivors of violence, belief in a kind and loving God can become difficult."

"That's so true," said Tom. "These ideas have been transformative to those who've been victims of violence. A woman named Jamie sent me a letter about her abuse. She wondered why God wouldn't stop the horrors she endured."

I shook my head. "That poor woman."

Tom nodded. "But hearing that a loving God can't control others helped her to see that God wasn't to blame. God neither caused her abuse nor permitted others to do it, as if God could've stopped them."

"I like ideas that aren't just head games, but have practical, real-world value."

"Right, and I could tell many more stories," said Tom. "These ideas aren't just good theoretical explanations for God and evil. They really make a difference in how real people live their lives."

"And that's the most important thing," I said. "That's one of the main problems with many explanations of the problem of evil."

"Right, if you think God is in control, you have to think God wanted every rape, torture, genocide, war, and more. And that just doesn't make sense to me. I can't imagine a loving God wanting the evils so many have suffered in history."

A little lizard walked over my hiking boot, paused for a moment on top, and then scurried off to find his breakfast. I looked at Tom. "What are your thoughts about natural evil? What about natural events that cause so much suffering?"

Tom nodded. "I think this view applies not only to the evil that freewill creatures do to one another. It also applies to evils like earthquakes, hurricanes, and tornadoes. I don't think those natural phenomena are caused by free will."

"No, I wouldn't think so."

"But I think God loves even the smallest particles of reality." Tom looked at me. "And God's love for those particles is uncontrolling. So, when random events occur, accidents happen, mutations occur in our genes, or even randomness occurs at the quantum level, God isn't controlling."

"God doesn't cause natural disasters," I said, "but God does work in the hearts and hands of those trying to help afterward."

He nodded. "To put it another way, God's uncontrolling love is expressed to the most complex creatures like you and me and the least complex objects at the micro-level of existence."

"God loves everyone and everything," I said, "from the tiniest particle to the entire universe."

"And that love is uncontrolling."

"God doesn't choose to love in this way," I said, processing the implications of these ideas. "God's very *nature* is uncontrolling love. That's who God is."

"That's right."

Looking up at the birds circling overhead, I thought in silence for a moment. I looked back at Tom. "I spend a lot of time praying. It comes as naturally to me as breathing. If God is always uncontrolling, does prayer still have value?"

"Oh yes," said Tom. "Our prayers become data and information God can use. And because God can't control others, our praying can be used to bring about good in the world."

I nodded my head. "Prayer opens up new ways for God to work. Prayer changes us. And prayer changes the things we are praying about for the better."

"Yes," said Tom. "Prayer makes a difference, but it doesn't control."

"So, to summarize," I said. "God is always active, always loving, but never controlling."

"Yes," said Tom. "That's why we need to say God *can't* prevent evil rather than God *won't* prevent evil."

Tom had given me a lot to think about. Regardless of whether he was ultimately right or wrong, our conversation inspired me to think more about love as an answer to the problem of evil. Picking up my knapsack, I shook his hand and thanked him for his time. Tom gathered his gear to move to another area to take more pictures, and I turned and began the long hike down the trail.

As I walked, my thoughts circled around God and love. *The power of God is the power of love. But the power of love is a different kind of power than most human ideas of power*. I thought about the power of Christ versus the power of Caesar. The power of peace versus the power of guns, bombs, and armies. The power of compassion versus the power of cyanide. *Love is the most powerful force in the universe*, I thought, *but it's a different kind of power. The power of God is the power of love. God is always active, always loving, always working to squeeze every drop of good possible out of every situation.*

I rested my right foot on a boulder and tied my hiking boot. In the distance, I could see the entrance to the parking lot where I had left my car.

God loves everyone and everything, I thought as I hiked down the trail towards the parking lot. *God loves every person and every particle of existence.* I stepped over a fallen tree and saw a candy-bar wrapper left by another hiker. I picked it up and put it in my pocket to throw away later. My mind continued to muse: *God loves whoever left this wrapper. God loves good people and God loves bad people. God loves nature and God loves animals. God loves victims and God loves their families.* An image of the murdered woman I found when I was five years old flashed into my mind, and compassion filled my heart. *God loves that woman,* I thought. *She's safe in heaven now, where there's a different and better way of being.* Those insights were easy. But the next awareness was harder. I swallowed hard, realizing the terrifying love of God. *God loves the Pain Killer, whoever that is ...*

A strange warmth filled my heart. Waves of love, compassion, and forgiveness swept over me. In a flash, the love of God ignited within me. Suddenly, I saw John Price through fresh eyes. Although I by no means condoned his actions, I felt compassion for a fellow human being who had suffered a very difficult childhood. Someone whose parents abandoned him at a transient motel when he was a toddler. Someone who struggled with mental illness and was raised in extreme poverty. I felt empathy for both John and Sarah Price—two parents who lost their only child in a terrible, horrible way, and couldn't have another. A couple who loved each other and stayed together, despite all the pain they had endured. A husband who felt his wife was cheated by her boss, and in a moment of madness felt compelled to avenge her by writing the extortion letter. A man who made terrible choices, but didn't know what else to do. And hopefully, a man who deeply regretted his many mistakes.

I don't know who the Pain Killer is, I thought as I walked toward my car, *but I do know one thing*.

An eagle piped a single, high-pitched note overhead, drawing my eyes towards heaven. Something released within me. Tears of joy, and peace, and love, and healing flowed down my cheeks. I cried aloud to the gentle clouds sailing like ships across the sea-blue sky.

"God loves John and Sarah Price."

EPILOGUE
FORGIVENESS IS THE BEST REVENGE

A shooting star blazed towards the earth, like Satan falling from heaven. Stirring the dying embers of my campfire with a hickory stick, I thought back to all that happened. The warmth of my campfire embraced me in the darkness of the frosty night, and thoughts floated across my mind.

Years have passed, my children have grown, and they have become amazing people of whom I am so proud. I continued working in ministry, and remained the sole provider for our family. But we went through a great trial. We discovered that my wife and their mother, Eve, was having an online affair with a Nigerian "romance scammer." He gained her confidence, and then he began asking her to send him large sums of our family's money. Before I discovered her actions, she secretly transferred to him several payments of several thousands of dollars each. This was money I had earned and earmarked for our children's future. This situation led to a painful divorce, but my children and I have continued on as a loving family.

I've learned that forgiveness is the best revenge. But forgiveness doesn't mean letting the hurt go on and on.

I forgive her, I wish her well, and I release her from my life.

As I gazed at the dying embers of the campfire, I thought of my new book about the Chicago Tylenol Murders and how it relates to the mystery of evil. I had finished the rough draft, and I ran over the contents in my mind.

If this was a movie, I would tie up many loose ends about the plot. There would be a clear-cut solution to the murders, and I would answer every remaining question. But this is real life and not a movie. And in real life, ambiguity and the unknown are facts of life.

Why did my parents seem to underreact about everything that happened? My only answer is that they thought the best of everyone, including John and Sarah Price. I asked my mother recently, "Didn't any of what John and Sarah said and did strike you as strange?" And my mother said, "Well, it does now. But that was a different time. The world has forever changed for the worse. And it was John and Sarah who changed it."

Although decades have passed since the terrible events of 1982, police have never solved the Chicago Tylenol Murders. It is still an active case. But even though this murder mystery is still unsolved, we have explored a deeper mystery in this book. We have discovered a plausible answer to the question: *If God is good, why is there so much evil in the world?*

We have learned that God is the most powerful, the most loving, and the most active Being in existence. But there are some things even God *can't* do singlehandedly. And there is a big difference between God *can't* and God *won't*. God couldn't stop a madman from placing cyanide poison in Tylenol capsules. Or keep Jim Jones from deluding so many. Or stop my former wife from sending our children's money to a romance scammer in Nigeria.

As my friend Tom Oord would say, God's essential nature is uncontrolling love, and God loves everyone and everything. And so, God *can't* force anyone to do anything. It's not that God doesn't want to stop all evil, it's that God can't do so singlehandedly. But God *can* work to wring every drop of good possible out of bad situations that God doesn't want in the first place.

But why can't God stop evil singlehandedly?

God can't do these things singlehandedly, because God's very nature is uncontrolling love. God is not constrained by any outside force or principle, but by God's own nature. In the words of the New Testament, *God cannot deny himself* (2 Timothy 2:13). God needs our help to accomplish God's will. God needs our cooperation to stop crime. God calls us to freely choose to resist evil, make ethical choices, and help those who are victims of crime. God can't make us do these things, and God can't do these things alone.

But God *can* love us, God can inspire us, God can encourage us, and God can give us strength to get through the hard times. And that makes all the difference.

And so, we end both with a solution and a mystery.

Will these horrible crimes ever be solved? Who is the person I call the *Pain Killer*? Was John Price the perpetrator of the murders? The truth is, we may never know. Somewhere out there, someone knows the truth behind the Chicago Tylenol Murders. I hope that my book will be part of the solution to these terrible crimes. I hope that if any readers have any information regarding this case, they notify the FBI immediately.

John Price was charged with extortion, served time, and is now a free man. He was never charged with the actual Tylenol murders, but he remains in the minds of many the prime suspect to this day. He and his wife are still married and only they know for sure the extent of their involvement with the Tylenol murders.

Their marriage has lasted, but mine has crumbled.

As with my ex-wife, I forgive them, I wish them well, and I release them from my life.

My parents trusted John and Sarah Price too much.

I trusted my ex-wife too much.

But I've learned something important in the process. Bad things can and do happen in life, and they are not our fault. Some things are out of our control. But what is within our control is how we react to what has happened to us. Even in the most difficult things in life, we can find meaning and wisdom. We can use them as opportunities for personal growth and spiritual transformation. We can become better people in spite of the pain and suffering of life. We can discover an alchemy of the soul, and transform the lead of our misfortunes into spiritual gold. Even great pain and betrayal can provide the necessary spur to spark enlightenment.

As the final puffs of hickory smoke haunted the night air, I watched the last ember of my campfire fade into nothingness. Gazing up at the glory of the stars, I realized my oneness with all life. The universe itself was my body. My true spiritual nature was the string upon which the galaxy was strung, and the stars were the pearls. My individual self both diminished and expanded at the same time. I was no longer a being, but pure being itself.

The half-smile of an enlightened master spread across my face.

The danger had passed.

Peace had come.

I was finally free.

Appendix A: Sources, Resources, and Further Reading

Chicago Tylenol Murders

The Chicago Tylenol Murders have been well documented in a broad variety of publications. In the days following the murders, a hundred-thousand articles were published. During that same time, the case had the most news coverage of any event since the assassination of John F. Kennedy. And so, there is a vast number of resources about this event, and it is not possible to list them all here. The author has tried diligently to consult multiple quality sources, including books, articles, videos, podcasts and personal interviews. Some of these sources had conflicting information, and the author had to work in the context of those ambiguities. The following are a few of the better sources the author found while doing research for this book. The reader is invited to read these original sources for a fuller picture of the Tylenol Murders. Readers are encouraged to do their own research and come to their own conclusions. Since the author was only a small child at the point when this story begins, he also relied heavily on family memories to augment and fill in his personal memories. Most significant in this regard was the information given to the author by his parents, especially his father.

Books, Articles, and Other Sources

The Tylenol Mafia: Marketing, Murder, and Johnson & Johnson by Scott Bartz.
The Tylenol Mafia is a book about the Chicago Tylenol Murders. The individual who was arrested and later convicted of writing the Tylenol extortion letter to Johnson & Johnson has a link to the *The Tylenol Mafia* on his website. That same individual gives a positive review of Bartz's book, recommends visitors to his website to "order it and read it," and he also gave email interviews used in *The Tylenol Mafia*. Due to these factors, *The Tylenol Mafia* would seem to be an excellent resource for getting his side of the story. My hope is that reading *The Tylenol Mafia* will help the reader of my book find a balanced and fair view of the events and suspects, so they can consider all sides and make their own informed opinion.

Other helpful reading and sources include:

Bergmann, Joy (November 2, 2000). "A Bitter Pill." Chicago Reader. Retrieved September 3rd,

2021. This is an excellent article and highly recommended.

"Feds Convinced Lewis Was Tylenol Killer." WCVB-TV. February 12, 2009. Archived from the original on October 30, 2011. Retrieved September 3rd, 2021.

Lavoie, Denise (January 11, 2010). "Friend: Tylenol Suspect Submits DNA, Fingerprints." Associated Press (via ABC News). Archived from the original on December 5, 2014. Retrieved September 3rd, 2021.

"Tylenol Figure Is Convicted." Associated Press (via The New York Times). January 15, 1984. Archived from the original on March 5, 2016. Retrieved September 3rd, 2021.

Douglas, John E.; Olshaker, Mark (1999). The Anatomy of Motive –The FBI's Legendary Mindhunter Explores the Key to Understanding and Catching Violent Criminals. New York City: Scribner. ISBN 978-0-684-84598-2.

"The trail of The Tylenol Man." Boston.com. February 6, 2009. Archived from the original on March 27, 2019. Retrieved September 3rd, 2021.

"Case 118: The Chicago Tylenol Murders." Casefile: True Crime Podcast. July 21, 2019. Archived from the original on October 12, 2019. Retrieved September 3rd, 2021.

"FBI Searches Home of Man Linked to Tylenol Deaths." Fox News. Associated Press. February 4, 2009. Archived from the original on August 19, 2014. Retrieved September 3rd, 2021.

Saltzman, Jonathan (February 5, 2009), "Fatal Tampering Case Is Renewed", The Boston Globe, archived from the original on May 16, 2010, retrieved September 3rd, 2021.

Fletcher, Dan (February 9, 2009). "A Brief History of the Tylenol Poisonings." TIME. Archived from the original on January 20, 2018. Retrieved September 3rd, 2021.

Fifis, Fran (February 5, 2009). "Law Enforcement To Review Tylenol Murders." CNN. Archived from the original on April 15, 2009. Retrieved September 3rd, 2021.

"Remembering the Victims of the Chicago Tylenol Murders." Beyond the Dash. October 16, 2020. Retrieved September 3rd, 2021.

Wikipedia contributors. "Chicago Tylenol murders." Wikipedia, The Free Encyclopedia. Wikipedia, The Free Encyclopedia, 23 Aug. 2021. Web. 3 Sep. 2021.

APPENDIX B: Self-help, Psychology, and Spirituality

If you are dealing with any mental or emotional health issue, please contact your doctor right away. For a referral, please call SAMHSA's National Helpline. This hotline is a 24/7, 365-day-a-year treatment referral and information service (in English and Spanish) for individuals and families facing mental and/or substance use disorders. SAMHSA's National Helpline is 1-800-662-HELP (4357).

For a self-help book on anxiety and depression, I recommend the following:

Unlearning Anxiety & Depression: The 4-Step Self-Coaching Program to Reclaim Your Life by Joseph J. Luciani, PhD.

Feeling Good by David Burns, M.D.

To explore the psychology of evil, I recommend:

People of the Lie by M. Scott Peck.

For general reading concerning pain, loss, evil, and suffering, I recommend:

When Bad Things Happen to Good People by Harold S. Kushner

A Grief Observed by C.S. Lewis

The Problem of Pain by C.S. Lewis

To learn more about the Principalities and Powers discussed in Chapter 20, I recommend the following:

God at War by Gregory Boyd. If you only read one book on this subject, this should be it. I am indebted to Boyd's work for enriching my thinking on what Boyd calls the Warfare Worldview.

The Powers That Be by Walter Wink. This short summary of Wink's excellent work presents a different view of the Powers.

The Screwtape Letters by C.S. Lewis. A fictional exploration of the Powers with practical applications.

The Unseen Realm: Recovering the Supernatural Worldview of the Bible by Michael S. Heiser. A scholarly book that is still accessible to the non-specialist.

And of course, the *Holy Bible* (the *English Standard Version* is currently the best for a study of the Powers).

For a study bible with excellent notes about the Powers, I recommend the *Faithlife Study Bible*, by the makers of *Logos Bible Software*. Some study bibles have similar names; this particular one can be identified by noting Michael S. Heiser (author of *The Unseen Realm* and other similar books) is one of the contributors. At time of publication, there is also a free app of this excellent study bible available.

Finally, to further explore Essential Kenosis and the theology of God's uncontrolling love, I recommend the work of theologian, philosopher, and scholar Thomas Jay Oord, Ph.D., whom we met in Chapter 21. Especially relevant to understanding evil and suffering are the following:

God Can't: How to Believe in God and Love after Tragedy, Abuse, and Other Evils. This is the book to begin with for most readers.

Questions and Answers for God Can't. A Q&A book to further expand on the material in the first book.

The Uncontrolling Love of God: An Open and Relational Account of Providence. This book is more academic and scholarly than the previous two books listed here.

Partnering with God: Exploring Collaboration in Open and Relational Theology. Dr. Oord is one of the editors of this excellent volume of essays. I have an essay in *Partnering with God* entitled "God's Fellow Workers" (page 341).

APPENDIX C: Report Threats and Crime

If you or someone else is in imminent danger, call 911 or your local police immediately.

If you are dealing with internet scams, romance scams, or any of the many Nigerian scams, do not send them money, and report this criminal activity right away at: https://www.ic3.gov/

Although the Tylenol Tip Line was closed after the prime suspect's arrest, you can and should still notify the FBI if you have any information regarding this case.

If you have a non-emergency tip regarding the Chicago Tylenol or other major crime, the following are three ways to inform the FBI:

Contact your local FBI office or closest international office 24 hours a day, seven days a week.

Call 1-800-CALLFBI (225-5324) for the Major Case Contact Center.

You can also contact them online through the FBI Website: https://www.fbi.gov/tips

AUTHOR'S NOTE

Please read the following Legal Disclaimer. The reader understands the following: Although based on actual events, this book is a dramatization and written in the literary form of a novel. As such, it should be interpreted as literature. Some names, characteristics, dates, locations, occupations, and other details have been changed to protect privacy. The names "John and Sarah Price" are fictional, and are not the real names of any suspects of the Chicago Tylenol Murders, or of any other crime. Any similar names in the real world are strictly coincidental, and unrelated to the fictional use of these names in this novel. Furthermore, "John and Sarah Price" are composite literary characters and are not to be misconstrued as literal representations of any certain person or persons, living or dead; this is true about other characters in this book as well, including but not limited to Jack's wife, Eve. Some events in this novel have been compressed, some characters are composite or fictional, and some dialogue has been added, created, or recreated. No dialogue contained in this novel should be construed as direct quotes or admission of guilt. The conversations in this book are not written to represent word-for-word transcripts. Characters in this novel are portrayed fictionally, poetic license is used throughout, and certain people portrayed in this novel may have memories of the events that differ from the author or reports given to the author. The author is telling his own personal and family story to further the public interest and to help victims of crimes and violence deal with emotional pain. The author's primary sources for the personal events related in this novel are both personal and family memories, as well as the reports of others involved, reported to the author many years after the original events; in an effort to be as fair and accurate as possible, these have been integrated with published material, public documents, court records, etc., involving the actual events upon which this novel is based. In many cases, the sources interviewed or consulted could not remember the exact words said by certain people, or exact descriptions of certain things, and so the author had to use creativity to fill in gaps. To create a more complete representation of certain events, some characters share information that was actually reported at a later date through published sources. For literary purposes, the author has put the narrator into some reported situations and events where he was not physically present at the time, and therefore not an eyewitness; these events were recreated based on the reports of those who were present. This novel reflects the author's present recollections of those reports, early childhood experiences, and the reported experiences of others, as conveyed to the author over many decades of research. The author acknowledges that decades-old memories can be faulty, are subjective, and should not be taken as fact or eyewitness testimony. Reflections, comments, and observations contained within this novel are the personal opinion of the author and/or his sources, and nothing more. Furthermore, the author has no malice against anyone, living or dead. Although the author has tried diligently to ensure that the information in this book was correct at the time it was published, the author does not in any way assume and hereby disclaims any liability to any party for any loss, damage, libel, defamation, or disruption caused by errors, opinions, or omissions, whether these errors, opinions, or omissions were the results from negligence, accident, faulty reporting, or any other cause whatsoever. All suspects and all statements concerning all events mentioned in this book are merely opinion and hereby qualified as "alleged." Being a novel inspired by actual events and not a news article, a certain amount of dramatic license, selective characterization, symbolism, and plot devices have been used to create a more coherent narrative. It is not a comprehensive representation of the whole case, all the people involved, or the entire investigation, and therefore should not be interpreted as such. It is presented from a single narrator's perspective, and is just one possible retelling of the events surrounding this case. The author does not accuse any specific person or persons of committing the crimes related in this book, or of any other crime whatsoever. The author takes no responsibility for the statements and reports made to him upon which this novel is based, but has tried to relate that information faithfully as received. This novel has not been approved, endorsed, edited, or authorized by any law enforcement agency. It is the author's hope that this book will help those who have suffered loss, crime, betrayal, or violence, and the intention of the author is to help these readers find faith, hope, and meaning after tragic events. Nevertheless, the content of this book is for informational purposes only. It is not intended to diagnose, treat, cure, or prevent any condition or disease. The reader understands that this book is not intended as a substitute for consultation with a licensed practitioner or medical professional. Please consult with your own physician, pastoral counselor, psychologist, or healthcare specialist regarding the suggestions and recommendations made in this book. The use of this book implies your acceptance of this legal disclaimer.

ABOUT THE AUTHOR

The Rev'd Greg T. Hoover, an award-winning writer, is a professional actor, behavior therapist, and Episcopal priest. Greg loves the outdoors, hiking, traveling, and playing guitar. He is the author of *The Witching of the King*, a historical murder mystery novel featuring William Shakespeare as an amateur detective.

NOTE FROM THE AUTHOR

Word-of-mouth is crucial for any author to succeed. If you enjoyed *The Pain Killer*, please leave a review online—anywhere you are able. Even if it's just a sentence or two. It would make all the difference and would be very much appreciated.

    Thanks!
    Greg Hoover

We hope you enjoyed reading this title from:

www.blackrosewriting.com

Subscribe to our mailing list—*The Rosevine*—and receive **FREE** books, daily deals, and stay current with news about upcoming releases and our hottest authors.

Scan the QR code below to sign up.

Already a subscriber? Please accept a sincere thank you for being a fan of Black Rose Writing authors.

View other Black Rose Writing titles at www.blackrosewriting.com/books and use promo code **PRINT** to receive a **20% discount** when purchasing.

www.ingramcontent.com/pod-product-compliance
Lightning Source LLC
Chambersburg PA
CBHW071954070526
44583CB00015B/1189